guide

RHODES

RHODES

by John Bowman

EFSTATHIADIS GROUP

ISBN 960 226 210 9

Photography by A. Spyropoulos

Distributed by:
EFSTATHIADIS GROUP S.A.
Ag. Athanasiou Str. GR. 145 65 Anixi Attikis Tel. 8131593
14 Valtetsiou St. GR 106 80 Athens Tel. 3615011
34 Olympou-Diikitiriou St. GR. 546 30 Thessaloniki Tel. 51178

EFSTATHIADIS GROUP
Agiou Athanasiou St. Anixi Attikis, Tel. 813159
14 Valtetsiou St. Athens, Tel. 3615011
Bookshop: 84 Academias St. Tel. 3637439

The entrance to the harbour

CONTENTS

1 Preface

9

THE DODECANNESE: INTRODUCTION   9
THE PHYSICAL ENVIRONMENT   13
FORMATION OF THE DODECANNESE
   ISLANDS   13
THE CLIMATE OF THE DODECANNESE   15
ANIMAL LIFE   17
PLANT LIFE   17

2 Visiting Dodecannese

20

WHEN WE GO   20
TIME FOR THE DODECANNESE   23
TRAVELING AROUND THE DODECANNESE   26
TRAVELLING ON THE DODECANNESE   31
ACTIVITIES & DIVERSIONS   33
SPORTS & OUTDOOR ACTIVITIES   33
FESTIVALS   36
TRADITIONAL POPULAR CULTURE   38
PROFESSIONAL ENTERTAINTMENT   40
CRAFTS & SHOPPING   40
EATING & DRINKING   42

3 Rhodes

45

THE PHYSICAL PRESENCE   45
RHODES IN MYTH AND HISTORY   46
TRAVELING TO AND ON RHODES   56
ACCOMMODATIONS ON RHODES   57
ACTIVITIES AND DIVERSIONS   59

4 The City Of Rhodes

62

RHODES; OLD TOWN   65
THE MEDIEVAL WALLS OF RHODES   84
WRAPPING UP YOUR VISIT TO THE CITY
   OF RHODES   86

5 Lindos

90

THE DRIVE TO LINDOS   90
OTHER SITES ON RHODES   103
IALYSOS PETALOUDES KAMEIROS   103

PROFITIS ELIAS   108
KALLITHEA   110
KASTELLORIZO   110

6 General Practical Information from A to Z

112

7 A little Greek for travelers

132

BASIC DAILY SITUATIONS   133
NUMBERS   133
TIME   134
HOTEL   134
RESTAURANTS   135
AROUND TOWN   135
ON THE ROAD   136

1. Preface

The Dodecannese:
AN INTRODUCTION

An unusual word for an unusual locale. Many people, in fact, may not immediately recognize the word, although as soon as Rhodes is singled out, most people will respond positively. But this is ironic, since Rhodes was not actually a member of the original **Dodecannese,** while many people have quite specific links with two of the Dodecannese – **Kos** and **Patmos** – not to mention the fact that one of the roots of the word, **dodeka,** is one of the first Greek words everyone learns because it means "twelve", although in fact there are more than twelve islands in Dodecannese, which in any case were long known as the Southern **Sporades.** About the only thing that can simply be said is that they are a group of beautiful and interesting Greek islands in the eastern **Aegean.**

But to back up a bit and deal with the apparent paradoxes. The name of these islands, Dodecannese, means nothing more than "The Twelve Islands," but this term has no classical standing; indeed, it only was coined in 1908, when 12 islands that had enjoyed a "privileged" status under the Turks since the 16th century joined to protest the Turks withdrawal of certain privileges. Rhodes, Kos, and **Lipsoi,** now included in the Dodecannese, were not involved in this situation. But as their fate came to be entwined with the others in events following the Italo-Turkish war of 1911-12, these islands not only joined **"The Twelve";** Rhodes – always the largest and most influential island of this area – came to be the capital of the Greek administrative region, or Nome, now formally the Dodecannese. But there are 14 islands in the Nome that have independent local governments – **Rhodes, Telos, Syme, Chalki, Megisti, Kos, Nisyros, Karpathos, Kasos, Patmos, Lipsoi, Leros, Astypalaia,** and **Kalymnos** – (p.114,5, 130,1) while several of their dependent islets are also inhabited. As for the **Southern Sporades** – the latter word being Greek for "scattered islands" – this is seldom applied to any Aegean islands, at least by foreigners.

It is foreigners to whom this guide is primarily addressed, and whether this is the first visit to Greece or but one in many, this book is designed to make the Dodecannese as accessible and enjoyable as possible. Rhodes, of course, is one of the best-known "tourist spots" in the world, one of those distinctive places that has had centuries of experience

Eastern part of the Doric Stoa on the Acropolis of Lindos

View of Mahdraki and the new market from the Palace of the Grand Master

in providing hospitality – and sunshine –' for millions of visitors; before this guide is ended, it will have cast a fresh light on many of the old and new aspects of Rhodes. So, too, on Kos, home of the Sanctuary of **Aesclepius,** an ancient medical center, and of **Hippocrates,** the father of medicine and of the **Hippocratic Oath,** still taken by doctors

many little-known points of interest. For there is far more to these islands than is often publicized. There are discos, to be sure, but there is also bicycle riding; there are beaches, but there are traditional costumes; there are chic boutiques but there are also sponges; there are Greek and Turkish remains, but there are also **Crusader** and Italian

The Palace of the Grand Master

in many lands. And on Patmos, as well, where St. John the Divine received and then dictated the **Revelation.**

But these are merely the most obvious attractions of the Dodecannese, and it is the aim of this guide to illuminate the tremendous diversity of these islands, even to reveal

structures; there are bustling streets with souvenirs and grand hotels – even a casino, but there are remote villages following age-old patterns of life. All this and much more will be made accessible by this guide.

12

THE PHYSICAL ENVIRONMENT

Perhaps because these islands were never historically bound, but in any case because of their diversity, it makes more sense to provide the details of mythology, history, biography and such human dimensions under each individual island. But it is also true that the Dodecannese do share a geography, an environment, an ecology. And although not all visitors are interested in such matters in the abstract, they sooner or later must interact with these very real physical elements: if nothing else, the climate, the sea conditions, the terrain, the food and drink, all these are of immediate concern to even the most casual tourist.

FORMATION OF THE DODECANNESE ISLANDS

The ancients recounted various myths to explain the presence of individual islands such as Rhodes, but the modern geologist's explanation is in some ways even more intriguing. In this contemporary version, the formation of the Aegean world is a chapter in the larger story of the formation of the earth's major land and sea forms, one that goes back to at least 200,000,000 years ago. At that time there was a single mass of land on this planet; the land is now called Pangea and the surrounding sea is called Panthalassa (and thus do modern geologists pay tribute to the Greek mythological realm). A large bay extended across the area that would eventually become the Mediterranean, the Greek mainland, and all the way into the Middle East; this is now known as the Tethys Sea, and over millions of years great sediments were laid down over this sea's bottom (thus accounting for the fossils of marine organisms that may now be found on high land throughout the Aegean).

About 200,000,000 years ago, **Pangaea** began to break apart into two masses that in turn eventually split into the continents we know today. (This so-called drifting is explained by geologist's theory of plate tectonics.) All this took millions of years, during which time the **Tethys Sea** receded at its eastern end and became linked at the west to what became the Atlantic Ocean. By about 65,000,000 years ago the major movements had ceased and the shapes and locations of the continents were essentially those of our day. But the Aegean Sea and its islands still did not exist in their present forms; some scientists, in fact, believe that the entire Mediterranean Sea dried up at least a dozen times during this period as the water drained out into the Atlantic and then came back as the continents of Africa and Europe continued to open and close near the Strait of Gibraltar. Meanwhile, as the great plates moved against one another, they pushed up the great mountains that border the Mediterranean Sea as well as those mountains that would eventually surface as the islands of the Mediterranean.

For eventually the Mediterranean Sea receded to its present level, leaving the shorelines and islands much as they are today. In the last million years, however, and even in quite recent times, there have been minor adjustments: earthquakes, volcanoes, local subsidence and elevation, delta formation, erosions – all have contributed to shaping the Aegean world. But the major forms of the Dodecannese are explained by their being peaks of the vast submarine massif that is linked to the continents of Europe and Asia. The

Bouganvilaea

Dodecannese are actually remnants of the range that extends down through Greece, the Peloponnesos, Crete and over to the Turkish mainland. Because the African plate is still pushing against the Aegean plate, the land at its edges is relatively unstable so that there are volcanic islands (such as **Santorini** and **Nisyros)** and occasional earthquakes. But the visitor need hardly worry about either of these phenomena: the last earthquake of any consequence in the Dodecannese was one on Kos in 1933, while the last major earthquake on Rhodes was in 1863.

Most of the Dodecannese, like the other Aegean islands, are composed of limestone, a sedimentary rock laid down over millions of years when the Tethys Sea covered the entire area; there is also some flysch, a sedimentary deposit largely of sandstone. None of the Dodecannese can claim either the fine marbles or other minerals and metals that are found on some of the other Aegean islands, although there are some good local building stones.

The total land area of the Dodecannese – the 14 major islands and their dependencies – is some 2,700 sq. km, or about 1,064 sq m. (To give some sense of this, Crete alone is some 8,300 sq. km.) Rhodes itself constitutes over half the area – some 1,450 sq. km.

14

AVERAGE MONTHLY TEMPERATURES
IN CENTIGRADE

Months	Atmospheric Air of:		Sea Surface (1400 hrs) at:	
	Rhodes	**Athens**	**Rhodes**	**Ierapetra Crete**
JAN	11.6	9.3	14.8	17.1
FEB	12.0	10.0	14.9	16.2
MAR	13.3	14.4	15.5	16.9
APR	16.6	15.5	17.9	17.9
MAY	20.6	20.2	21.0	20.0
JUNE	25.0	24.7	24.2	22.3
JULY	27.2	27.5	25.9	24.2
AUG	27.6	24.6	25.4	24.8
SEPT	24.9	24.6	24.9	24.2
OCT	20.4	18.8	20.4	22.5
NOV	16.4	14.9	16.4	19.6
DEC	13.2	11.1	13.2	17.4

THE CLIMATE OF THE DODECANNESE

Although there is some slight variation in the weather on the Dodecannese – particularly in relation to the elevation – the islands generally enjoy a Mediterranean climate as defined by geographers, but with some sub-tropical elements. After all the technical details of the Mediterranean climate zone have been explained, it almost comes down to being one that will support olive trees, because what the olive tree needs is what the Dodecannese provide: hot, dry summers, clear if cool winters, and plenty of sunshine throughout the year. The Dodecannese boast of about 300 days when the sun can be seen. The summer is undeniably hot, but not the withering, enervating heat of the tropics. Winters can be cold at times, 15

The famous Bronze deer

but not so cold nor so extended that they require the diversion of large resources or energy. At higher elevations, of course, conditions differ, but neither the olive nor tourists are apt to be found there. There is virtually never frost or snow to be found on the Dodecannese, at least at sea level, and the winter rains tend to come and go quickly.

What makes the islands especially comfortable in the hot summer months are the breezes that come at different times of day and usually make summer nights quite bearable. In fact, from July through September, the steady wind from the northeast, known in Greece as the **meltemi,** keeps the whole Aegean quite refreshed, and even short inter-island hops by sea can sometimes be rough.

The fact that the Aegean is relatively isolated from the major oceans' patterns means that the water temperature around the Dodecannese remains somewhat higher at the surface than at depths; in the winter, however, the lower depths "hold" the upper layers to relatively higher temperatures (than would be true in the open sea). This relatively higher and more consistent surface temperature of the Aegean accounts for the mild winter temperatures – both water and air. But there is no use pretending that any except the most rugged will care to swim in the Dodecannese between October and May.

On the Dodecannese there are no freshwater lakes and no rivers or streams worth mentioning with the exception of a few on Rhodes, but there are numerous springs and some seasonal torrents on the larger islands. Rainfall is generally light and concentrated in the few months between September and May. But Rhodes is exceptionally green and fertile, and Kos, Leros, and Karpathos are also well-watered and support considerable vegetation. On several smaller islands, fresh water is a challenge for the inhabitants but never presents much of a problem to visitors. And there are some thermal spings and baths on Kos and Kalymnos.

ANIMAL LIFE

Except for the omnipresent birds and insects, the only animal life most visitors will be aware of on the Dodecannese will be the domesticated variety – sheep, chickens, pigs (and even these will be most present when served up on restaurant plates). The same holds true for the fish, although a visit to certain seaside markets should prove interesting. (And don't forget that the sponge is actually what remains of a marine animal, not a plant). The one island that has any exceptional animal populations is Rhodes. In addition to the famous butterflies (see page 104), there are some unexpected birds such as vultures, jays, and jackdaws. There are deer now running wild in a few locales, but the Italians re-introduced them earlier in this century. There are some small mammals – hare, badgers, martens, and foxes; there are some snakes (including one small poisonous species, but the chances of a typical visitor running into one of these are virtually nil); there is also among the usual Mediterranean lizards one unusually large species, – 12-14 inches long – **Agama stellio,** sometimes called 'the Rhodes dragon' but actually a hardun that is common throughout the Nile Delta.

PLANT LIFE

The cultivated plant forms of the Dodecannese are the usual ones of the Mediterranean – the olive, the grape, the fig, wheat and some other cereal grains, all the familiar vegetables and fruits; the only unfamiliar ones to many visitors might be the carob trees, some tobacco grown on a couple of islands, the pistacchio trees of Rhodes, and a variety of lettuce from Kos. But the real delight, if not surprise, comes from the wild vegetation. The trees, again, are not that unexpected – the pines, cypress, juniper, holm oak, some chestnut: likewise, the basic ground-cover is the familiar **maquis** of much of the Mediterranean – the tough, 17

scrublike plants and evergreen shrubs, including thyme, broom cistus, mock privet, and so many other species. Some islands are really quite green and fertile – Rhodes and Kos, for instance – while others of the Dodecannese are quite arid and barren, but all can boast of some wildflowers. There are the anemones and poppies, the wild marguerites, fennel, chamomile, several orchids, and many bulbs and tubers such as crocus, gladiolus, sternbergia, and cyclamen; on higher ground are found such lovely specimens as lilies, honeysuckle, hawthorne, peonies, and primrose. But of the over 6.000 wildflower species known to grow in Greece, some are found mainly in the Dodecannese or on the Greek islands off the coast of Turkey – one such being the **Ferula chiliantha,** a close relative of the plant whose stems the Sicilians use to make "cane" furniture. There is the **Paeonia Rhodia** Stearn, for instance, a peony endemic to Rhodes. And there are plants such as the **Hyoscyamus aureus,** a henbane, and **Lithospermum fruticosum,** a shrubby gromwell, both found mostly on Rhodes and Crete. All in all, whether visitors simply enjoy the colourful flowers or wish to identify them, there are plenty of species throughout the Dodecannese to keep happy.

Scenes from the island of Kos

2. Visiting Dodecannese

WHEN WE GO

Although most people have relatively little choice when it comes to the time period for their vacation, there are two main factors that should be considered by anyone with any choice when considering the Dodecannese (and Greece in general). These two factors are clearly related: the weather and the crowds.

Weather: The Dodecannese, like most of Greece, boast of about 300 rain-free, sun-visible days a year, so avoiding long rainy spells or finding the sun is not the issue. To be sure, there is considerable variation throughout Greece as a whole – from Macedonia to Rhodes, say – and then again from sea-level locales to mountainous heights. But since most people stay close to the coast – and tend to concentrate in southern Greece – this is hardly the issue, either.

What must be stressed, rather, are (1) the fact that the Eastern Mediterranean and such islands as the Dodecannese are **not** in the tropics, and (2) the region is subject to occasional brisk winds. Because of the delightful climate that the Dodecannese enjoy for 6-8 months of the year, many people have the mistaken impression that they are like some tropical paradise: consult the chart on p. 15 ' to see what the average temperatures are throughout the year on Rhodes and you will see that both air and water cool down appreciably. The simple fact is that most people will not care to swim in the Dodecannese between October and May, and people looking for a sun-filled holiday will not find the islands much fun between November and March.

But if you are not seeking a holiday of the kind largerly spent on the beaches and in crowded cafes, these off-season months in the Dodecannese can be delightful. Spring is a relatively short season, but starting in March-April many flowers come into blossom and the air begins to warm. By June, in fact, the greens of the landscape begin to give way to browns and yellows – because of the sun-filled, rainless days so beloved by travelers – and there is often a dusty haze that settles over many of the islands. Not until October does the rain begin to bring back some of the green, and although the weather definitely cools down from November to March, it is not the bone-chilling cold of northern lands: the sun is seldom gone for long, clear blue skies are often present even if the air is a bit cool, and a light jacket allows you to move around. (A ship voyage on a cold winter's day, however, is something quite different.)

Then there are those winds. The Aegean from July to September is exposed to a fairly steady stream of air from the northeast, what the modern Greeks know as the **meltemi**. This prevailing wind help relieve what might be a quite oppressive heat during these months and generally refreshes, the atmosphere. But the meltemi also makes for fairly choppy seas on occasion: it comes of something as a surprise to many travelers throughout the Aegean that relatively short sea trips can be relatively rough. But all the people operating the ships know and respect these conditions and smaller boats simply don't put to sea when things are too rough.

Crowds: Since these weather conditions are generally known to those in the world of tourism, it is no coincidence that most people converge on the Dodecannese from June through July and August. And in more recent years, so many people have been trying to avoid these peak months that even May and September are fairly busy. But aside from the impact of such numbers of foreigners on the Dodecannese and their inhabitants, do such crowds really affect other visitors?

Decidedly yes! For one thing, they can definitely fill up all the hotels on such islands as Rhodes, Patmos, and Kos so if you are particu-lar about your room you must make advance reservations. Otherwise you might well have to stay in far less classy and far more remote hotels, or even in rooms in private homes – and although many of these can be quite comfortable and plea-sant, they may not be to everyone's taste. Young people probably won't care if they have to bed down once in awhile on a floor or bunk or even sit through the night on a cafe chair, but not everyone will go for this. So to repeat: for high season – say, June-July-August – on Rhodes, Kos, Patmos at least, make reservations in advance if you require particular accommo-dations.

As for food and drink, although the islands have never been known to run out of them, there is no denying that restaurants and cafes can become very crowded during the peak months. What this means is that you must often wait to be seated and served, that when service comes it is often hasty, and that often items on a menu are sold out. But again: no one goes hungry or thirsty.

Meanwhile, transportation facilities can also become crowded during these peak months. If you can afford 1st or 2nd class, you can probably avoid most of these situations. And many people who travel around the Greek islands find the crowds part of the pleasu-re. Even so, you might want to

20

avoid certain especially crowded occasions: for instance, Easter weekend; on the days around August 15, when many Greeks make pilgrimages to Tinos and Paros; and near the end of August and early in September, when many people all head for Piraeus and Athens as the summer begins to close.

So where does this leave the visitor to the Dodecannese – and the Greek islands in general? If you come too early, not only will the water be too cold for swimming but many of the touristic facilities won't be operating – outdoor restaurants, for instance, may not have opened, archaeological sites and museums might be on reduced hours, there won't be as many ships or planes to choose from. But the lack of crowds might well compensate for these, at least for some travelers. Furthermore, not all islands attract such crowds even in the peak season, so one possibility is simply to avoid such places as Rhodes, Kos or Patmos during the peak season – or at least pass through them during a day or so and go on to less crowded islands.

But in the end, you must go to the Dodecannese when you want to and you will find – and make – the holiday you want. Whenever you go, though, travel light, with as little luggage as possible, and you will find everything about your trip goes easier.

Windsurfing

TIME FOR
THE DODECANNESE

Some people's ideal Greek holiday is to see as many of the cities and sites and islands as possible within a set period of time; other people's ideal would be to spend three weeks lounging about Rhodes. Between such extremes would fall most people's ideal holiday. In any case, this guide can be used to make any of these ideals more possible and pleasant. As indicated elsewhere, much depends on the time, money, and energy you are willing to spend: thus, air travel to the more distant points obviously frees a lot of hours for sunbathing or sightseeing.

Here are some suggestions about how to use your time in the Dodecannese. It is assumed that you are setting out from Athens or Piraeus.

3-7 Days: Most people will probably want to head first to Rhodes: perhaps this is the occasion to indulge in an airplane ticket, as the ship passage consumes 18 hours **each way** (although many of those hours are during sleeping hours and saving you hotel fees). But with even 3-7 days on the islands themselves, you'd still have time for only about one or two others besides Rhodes: Kos and Patmos are the most obvious goals; Karpathos might be more interesting to some (and could be visited enroute to Crete); or go up to Kalymnos (and then straight on to other Aegean islands or Piraeus).

8-14 Days: Time enough to see several of the Dodecannese beyond Rhodes (3-4 days); Kos (2 days); Patmos (1 day); Karpathos (2 days); Kalymnos (2 days). Pick out a couple of the smaller and less frequented islands (from the descriptions that follow in this guide); if you combine ships' schedules, you can make your way along several routes and get on to Crete or Samos or even to some foreign port.

15+ Days: If you were determined to do so, you could probably see all of the 14 major Dodecannese in 15 or so days, but this wouldn't allow you much time to explore as a lot of your time would be spent on ships. Not every island can be gotten into and out of every day, so it would take a lot of careful planning to make sure you don't get stuck on one of the less exciting islands for a disproportionate amount of time.

Even the air links between Rhodes and Kos, Karpathos, and Kassos won't save you all that many hours. Better to select a half dozen islands that appeal to you and concentrate on these.

TRAVELING AROUND THE DODECANNESE

Traveling to and from and among the Dodecannese is both more easily accomplished, if more difficult to explain, than is generally realized. This section will explain these apparent contradictions. In particular, it will dispel one current traveler's tale: that you can't move around the Greek islands, including the Dodecannese, without constantly returning to Piraeus.

AIR

Most travelers in the Aegean will not be using the air service – whether because it is too expensive or too unromantic– but for those with more money than time air connections with the Dodecannese offer a definite convenience; consider that the ship passage from Piraeus to Rhodes requires a solid 18 hours, while flight time is barely 1 hour. As for the comparative costs, they change often from year to year that it is confusing to give actual figures; but it is fair to say that air fares are less than first class on the ships, anywhere from about twice to just one-quarter more than second class (as ship fares vary greatly) dependent on the type of ship, traffic volume, etc.), and from about twice to three-quarters more than tourist class. Since people who travel first class tend not to worry about such costs, this may not be a factor; for others, what it means is that you end up paying about twice as much to get to some island while saving quite a few hours.

In any case, there are air connections to only a few of the Dodecannese. Except for charter flights to Rhodes – almost always part of package tours that require you to stay in particular hotels, etc. – there are no air links to cities outside Greece. The air links to the Dodecannese, therefore, are all by the Greek national airline, Olympic Airways; they all originate or end at the Athens-Hellinikon Airport, and actually most use Rhodes as the other terminus. There are about 5-6 flights daily each way between Athens and Rhodes.

There has also been one direct flight each way daily between Athens and Kos. Kos is also linked by Olympic to Rhodes. So, too, are Karpathos and Kassos linked to Rhodes. And Rhodes is also linked to Crete (Iraklion) by air. Once on Crete, you could make air connections with Santorini or Mykonos. But in general you cannot "fly around" the Dodecannese; even the links to Kos, Karpathos, and Kassos do not offer enough choices to allow you to get in and out on the most

A view of the City of Kos with the harbour

convenient schedules. On the other hand, in combination with the ship links, you can get around the Dodecannese using these air links.

As these schedules often change, and as many travel agents do not keep up with them, it is better not to try to make overly detailed plans from abroad; wait till you get to Greece, then go to the Olympic Airways or travel agent office, and plan your trip through the Dodecannese just before you are set to go.

SHIPS

From non-Greek ports: For most visitors this is not a possibility. But there are, in fact, several ways to get to the Dodecannese by ship from foreign ports. These are usually some ships that connect Rhodes to Alexandria, Egypt; Rhodes to Beirut, Lebanon, to Lattakia, Syria, and to Limassol, Cyprus; and there are even ships that connect Rhodes to Haifa, Israel, Dubrovnik, Yugoslavia, and to Venice, Italy. Such ships are not cheap, but they are certainly a delightful way of getting around the Mediterranean.

Then there are the cruise ships that might originate from some foreign port and put into at least Rhodes: but with only occasional exceptions, no one is allowed to leave these cruises and remain behind on the Greek islands. (For one thing, if you "jump ship," you won't have a proper passport clearance and you could have considerable trouble when you come to leave Greece.) There is the possibility that some freighter might be able to sell passage from one foreign port to one or another of the larger Dodecannese, but this would be an unusual situation. And of course privately owned or rented yachts may naturally sail into Greek waters and the Dodecannese ports. (Kos and Rhodes are the official ports of entry for passport and customs control).

Piraeus - Athens and the Dodecannese: Again, there are the cruise ships and yachts, but these will not answer most people's needs. Most people, rather, are simply interested in sailing direct from Piraeus to the Dodecannese. And there are indeed several possibilities. At least a couple times a week there has been one ship connecting direct to Rhodes. But there are other lines that go via other Greek islands and put in at Rhodes and other Dodecannese ports: one line has stopped at **Paros, Naxos, Ios, Santorini, Crete (Ayios Nikolaos** and **Sitia),** then at **Kassos** and **Karpathos** (including a second stop at Diafani), then on to **Halki,** the small island west of Rhodes, and finally on to Rhodes; another line goes via **Milos, Folegandros, Santorini, Crete** (Ayios Nikolaos and Sitia), and on to 27

28

Patmos

Kassos, Karpathos (including Diafani), **Halki,** and **Rhodes;** still another line goes via **Tinos, Patmos, Leros, Kalymnos,** Kos, and on to Rhodes.

So it is relatively easy to get ships to and from Piraeus and the main islands of the Dodecannese. Schedules change frequently, fares keep increasing, it is often hard to find out precise details from abroad. But the ship links are there.

Other Greek Ports: As will be apparent from the previous section – on ship links between Piraeus and the Dodecannese – several of the Dodecannese are linked to one another as well as to other Greek islands. But in addition to those main lines, there are numerous smaller ship lines that operate between and among the Dodecannese islands themselves: ships between Rhodes and such islands as **Syme, Tilos, Nissyros, Kos, Kalymnos, Kastelorizo, Karpathos, Kassos, Halki, Leros, Patmos,** and still others. So

once on one of the Dodecannese, you can usually get to the others by ship.

However, it is even more difficult to obtain precise and up-to-date information of schedules and fares about these ships when you are abroad – or for that matter in Athens. The National Tourist Organization has been known to issue weekly schedules and sometimes certain travel agents will be well informed. Best is simply to wait till you get to an island and then immediately ask the police or harbor master about ship connections. There's usually a local agent for the ship line, but be warned: they often will not volunteer information about competing lines and only grudgingly refer you to another agent. So keep your eyes and ears open while traveling the islands: other foreigners are often your best source of up-to-date information on these matters (because the local inhabitants, after all, are not that interested in island-hopping!)

Wild flowers of the Dodecannese

TRAVELLING ON
THE DODECANNESE

The means of getting about on the various islands vary greatly from Rhodes to the smallest, but one way or another you will be able to get to anywhere you wish. Since Rhodes offers an exceptional choice, there is a special discussion of its transportation facilities on p. 56. Here we discuss the general possibilities of the Dodecannese as a group.

PUBLIC BUS

All the major and sizeable Dodecannese have some public bus service – if only linking the main port to the main town: after all, the inhabitants have to get to and from ships, and often with large amounts of luggage. Not all the islands, however, can offer bus service to all the remote sites or monasteries, so you might have to walk a mile or two along a trail; also, schedules are not necessarily set for the convenience of the traveler who wants to spend a short time at a particular site and then move on. Thus some people might prefer one or another of the other possibilities discussed below.

TAXI

All except the smallest and least inhabited islands support at least a taxi, while the larger islands can provide quite adequate taxi service. For a small party anxious to see the more remote places in a minimum of time, a shared taxi is the best way to go. Or consider using a taxi in combination with the public bus when the latter's schedule is inconvenient. (For more about taxis, see that entry at Practical Information A to Z.)

CAR

Although it is possible to bring your own car on a ferry to many of the Dodecannese, it is a very expensive way to travel around these islands. Only a group of people intending to spend a fair amount of time traveling around Rhodes might find it economical – especially considering you have already paid to bring your car to Greece and might have to pay garage fees while on Rhodes.

Much more common is to rent a car – on Rhodes, that is. In recent years there has also been the possibility of renting a car on Kos and Kalymnos. Inquire when you get to Athens about the latest situation.

MOTORBIKE, SCOOTER, MOPED, BICYCLE

Increasing numbers of foreigners find these pleasant alternatives for getting around the islands, but it has only been Rhodes and Kos that

Windmills

have commercial rental firms. Kos is especially known for its bicycle rentals.

BOATS

On Rhodes, Patmos, Kos, and several of the other islands, there are boats that go to either remote beaches or sites (such as a monastery or a sea cave) or to nearby islets; such excursion boats dock along the main harbors of the main ports and clearly advertise their services. Rates are reasonable and the excursion can become a pleasant way of spending some time with some fellow travelers.

WALKING/ HITCHHIKING

Walking obviously remains – the last resort for many but the first resort to some. Especially on the smallest islands and for the more remote locales, it may be the only way. Overland trails by being a destination closer than it might seem by main roads, but then again overland trails are not for everyone. Meanwhile, hitchhiking (autostop) may appeal to some, but you cannot count on much traffic to the more remote locales.

ACTIVITIES & DIVERSIONS

Whether you head for the Dodecannese to see some particular historical or archaeological site or simply to enjoy the swimming and tavernas, there is much more to do on these islands than is generally known. We herewith offer some details about some of these possibly overlooked attractions of the Dodecannese.

SPORTS & OUTDOOR ACTIVITIES

For general remarks about sports and outdoor activities, look under these subjects in the section, "Practical Information A to Z": **Sports, Swimming, Underwater Sports, Yachting, Fishing, Hunting, Tennis.** Here we discuss aspects that apply more especially to the Dodecannese.

Swimming & Sunbathing: Swimming is a crucial element in the plans of many visitors to Greece so the section on "Swimming" (in Practical Information A to Z) should be read with special attention. It cannot be said too often: the water's temperature varies considerably from month to month (See Chart, p.15) and only the hardiest will want to swim in the waters around the Dodecannese between October and May. Only a few of the higher-class hotels on a few of the islands provide such amenities as changing rooms, showers, beach umbrellas, etc. And never underestimate the dangers of overexposure to the Aegean sun!

As for bathing or sunning in the nude, this has long been officially forbidden but unofficially overlooked, especially on several of the more isolated beaches tend to have a network

Windsurfing

Rowboating

of their own and keep informed of the possibilities. In any case, everyone should respect the local sensibilities as well as legarities.

As for the best of the beaches in the Dodecannese, these are identified and located on their respective islands in the accounts of specific islands.

Watersports: Except for a few of the expensive hotels on Rhodes and Kos, no one on the rest of the Dodecannese has been offering water-skiing, sail-surfing, paddleboats, or such activities (for hourly rates or fees). If you are determined to enjoy such sports, consult brochures of the best hotels and see what's available.

Underwater Swimming: Diving with SCUBA gear – portable oxygen apparatus – is forbidden on the Dodecannese (as throughout most of Gree-ce) unless special permission is obtained. But snorkel gear – the tube, mask, and flippers – is allowed everywhere. Underwater swimming might be forbidden at special archaeological sites (and near any military installations): these would be posted, and obviously underwater photography would also be forbidden at such locales. When in doubt, check with the local police or the nearest office of the **National Tourist Organization.**

Tennis & Golf: There are tennis courts on Rhodes and Kos that visitors may use, and there is a golf course on Rhodes open to the public.

Boating: The Dodecannese offer many fine harbors and sheltered bays to those who would like to move about the islands either by sailboats or power yachts: it is always

Sunbathing

taken for granted that no one would be so foolish as to set out without the proper knowledge and experience. Although the farthest distance between any of the Dodecannese headlands may be less than 100 miles, the winds and waves of the eastern Mediterranean can be unexpectedly dangerous. Almost anything can be rented on Rhodes, but a more reasonable alternative for most people would be to take one of the day excursions on several of the islands, small boats that take groups to more isolated beaches or sites. (These are described at the respective accounts of these islands.) Both Kos and Rhodes, by the way, are official points of entry and departure for boats entering Greece (for customs and passport control, that is).

Fishing & Hunting: There is no freshwater fishing to speak of on the Dodecannese, but there is obviously a lot of saltwater fishing. Foreigners may fish without any licence, but they may not fish in waters used by professional-commercial fishers. Underwater fishers may use a speargun, but not within 100 yards of public beaches.

As for hunting – which does require a licence and observe seasons – it is unlikely that anyone would travel to the Dodecannese to hunt the few small birds and mammals.

Mountaineering & Walking: No one would head for the

Dodecannese for challenging climbs, but Rhodes boasts of one respectable mountain, **Mt. Atavyros,** 1,215 meters (about 4,000 feet) and this has one marked trail from the village of Empona to the peak. Karpathos also has two respectable peaks: **Mt. Lastos** (or **Kalolimni**), about 3675 feet high, and **Mt. Profitis Elias,** about 3325 feet high. But there are many opportunities for walks around any of the islands. Just be sure you have proper footwear, sun-protection, clothing for cool times, and sufficient water and nourishment. Remember, too, that most of the land (and its produce) usually belongs to private individuals: you walk on their lands as a guest.

FESTIVALS

The general remarks about HOLIDAYS (in Practical Information A to Z) should be read in conjunction with this section; there are listed the major national holidays of all Greece, and many if not all of these are observed on the Dodecannese with appropriate festivities. (It also means that most facilities are closed on these days, so you must make your plans accordingly). But in addition to these national holidays, there are many special holidays and festivals that are observed on one or several of the Dodecannese, sometimes with more intensity than elsewhere; some people might like to schedule their visits to the appropriate islands to take advantage of this. Listed here are the better-known of such occasions on the Dodecannese. If you are especially interested in such occasions, ask at the local offices of the police, the National Tourist Organization, or even travel agencies as soon as you arrive on an island; with luck you'll run into someone who is going to celebrate a nameday or a wedding or a baptism in some village, and you may be invited to come along. Till then, here are some special occasions to attend on specific Dodecannese.

Dancing the local dances

Jan. 6
Many coastal locales, harbors, etc.
Epiphany ("12th Night") is celebrated all over Greece with rites blessing the sea.

Feb-Mar
Carnival: **Leros** especially, but at many places.
Carnival is a movable occasion (dependent on Easter) and is observed with various festivities.

Mar-April
Easter: **Patmos** above all, but everywhere.
For 3-4 days, all of Greece gives itself **Easter.**

April-May
Kalymnos: Find out when the sponge fleet will depart and attend the ceremonies.

April-Oct
Rhodes: City Sound & Light performances (in alternating languages) are given at the **Palace of the Grand Masters.**

Jun-Oct
Rhodes: City Performances of traditional dances by the Nelly Dimoglou Folk Dance Troupe, one of the oldest and best in all Greece.

Jun 21
Rhodes: Kalafonon: St. John's Day is observed with bonfires.

July-Aug
Rhodes: Valley of the Butterflies. Thousands of butterflies gather here and tourists gather to see them.

July-Sep
Rhodes: Rodini In this suburb of Rhodes City there is an annual and popular wine festival; in addition to featuring samples of the wines of Rhodes, it offers many foods and gifts.

July 17
Leros & Kassos The feast of **Ayia Marina** is especially observed on these two islands.

July 20
Kastellorizo Ascents of the mountains peaks, lighting fires, feasting and dancing -- all to celebrate the Prophet Elias -- throughout Greece but especially here.

July 27
Kalymnos The feast of **Ayios Panteleimon.**

Aug 14-23
Rhodes: Kremasti combines athletic events with religious ceremonies for miraculous icon of Virgin Mary.

Aug 15
Patmos, Nisiros, Astipalea: Assumption, or Dormition, of **Virgin Mary** is observed throughout Greece, but especially on **Patmos** and these other islands.

Sept 14
Khalki: Moni Stavros Exaltation of the Cross: the rites bless crop seeds.

Nov 7-9
Syme: Monastery of **St. Michael Panormitis** Feast of the Archangel Michael attracts pilgrims from all over area.

TRADITIONAL
POPULAR CULTURE

People have spent lifetimes trying to track down all the survivals of traditional and popular culture in the Greek world, but many visitors to the Dodecannese might be able to observe or participate in at least a few special occasions during even a limited stay. Here are some guideposts.

One of the best ways is to share in the traditional or special festivities listed on the calendar (p. 37). And even if you cannot time your visit to coincide with such events, there is always the possibility of attending a wedding or baptism or some such occasion when traditional music and dancing and feasting will play a role. Some of the islands have special songs and dances, of course. Kalymnos is noted for its bagpipes **(tsambouna)** and its expressive songs; Nisiros keeps alive traditional folk music, especially at the weddings and dances of Perioli on August 15; on Kos, at **Patani,** a few kilometers from Kos town, a Turkish community still gathers to play traditional Turkish music; Rhodes City offers bouzouki music, plus dancing at its Wine Festival, as well as the professional folkdance performances by the **Nelly Dimoglou** troupe. But music and dancing are seldom hard to come by anywhere in Greece.

Another approach for some might be to deliberately seek out those islands or villages where traditional ceremonies or traditions have been kept alive. Leros, for instance, observes Carnival in an unusual way: adults compose satirical verses that children dressed up as monks, recite at parties in homes where a marriage has occurred within the past year. (It is claimed that this can be traced back to ceremonies for **Dionysos** at Eleusis. The village of Olimbos on Karpathos is especially noted for maintaining its traditional clothes architectural style, a particular Doric dialect of Greek, and traditional costumes.

Those interested in traditional clothing, in fact, will have something of a festival of their own in the Dodecannese. In addition to Olimbos on Karpathos, where many of the inhabitants wear traditional clothing throughout the year, there is a town on Rhodes, Empona, where the inhabitants also wear traditional clothing everyday; and the women of **Tilos** wear traditional embroidered clothes much of the time; on Kassos, villagers wear traditional clothes on July 17, while those on Astipalea wear traditional clothing on August 15.

Yet another approach accessible to foreigners is to seek out every museum, collection, old house, or whatever that seems to have at least elements of the old and traditional. Lindos, on Rhodes, is usually passed through in a hurry by those on their way to its acropolis, but the town itself is a living museum of traditional medieval architecture. Rhodes City has the Papas Konstantinos House that is a museum of folk culture. Peek in old shops and you will often seek old textiles, ceramics, woodwork, metalwork, or such objects.

And if you are still determined to see more, inquire at the National Tourist Organization in each main city when you land on an island and someone should be able to direct you to any special locales or festivities. Remember, too, that many elements in the Orthodox Christian religion, especially as practices in the villages and countryside, can be traced to pre-Christian and pagan roots, so that you are experiencing a form of "living folklore" whenever you attend some religious occasion. If you speak Greek, of course, you will also be aware of how many traditional elements pervade the speech of Greeks – proverbs, superstitions, portents, catch phrases, and such. But the best way for most foreigners to share in the traditional culture of the Dodecannese is to attend some celebration or festival where music, dance, costumes, food, and various ceremonies all combine to present a true living folk culture.

PROFESSIONAL ENTERTAINTMENT

Those who need to be entertained by professional groups or individuals probably aren't travelling around the Dodecannese. But the fact is that the city of Rhodes does offer the Nelly Dimoglou Folk Dance Troupe, one of the oldest and finest in Greece, which performs between June and October; the city of Rhodes also offers a "Sound and Light" production from April to October. Professional musicians also pass through Rhodes and concertize on occasion. But that is about it for the Dodecannese. That still leaves discos or nightclubs with professional musicians and entertainers, and of course the movie theaters in large cities. And whether it is a sport or entertainment, there is the gambling casino in the city of Rhodes.

CRAFTS & SHOPPING

Most travelers through the Dodecannese, as elsewhere in Greece, look forward to taking

home some memento of this distinctive world, and there is no trouble finding shops that will sell you some souvenir. The problem is to find something that is truly indigenous and locally made. For the general problems of buying in Greece, see under SHOPPING & SOUVENIRS (in Practical Information A to Z); the Dodecannese present the same set of problems, especially when it comes to antiques. The best most visitors can hope for is a solid and tasteful and genuinely handmade object old or not.

There is one exception, however, to anything that is said about the Dodecannese: Rhodes. The city of Rhodes has been a magnet for so many tourists and travelers for so

Shopping for souvenirs

Handmade Carpets

long that its shops offer a dazzling selection of goods and gifts – probably the largest in Greece outside of Athens. But many of these items are not what most people come to the Dodecannese to purchase – tailor-made suits and dresses, expensive furs, jewelry, leather goods such as boots, even umbrellas and duty-free liquors. The main shopping district of Rhodes is a bazaar that should at least reward the window-shopper. But Rhodes does offer some indigenous goods: handmade carpets from Afandou, distinctive pottery and loomed textiles from Lindos.

So keep your judgment and wallet under control and you can find something to your taste. And follow the basic rules of souvenir-hunting throughout all of Greece: look around at first and get a sense of what's being offered at what prices, find something you like and can afford, then buy it and don't worry too much about its age – or source: a hardware store might have some item that appeals to you more than anything in the most expensive shop in Rhodes.

EATING & DRINKING

Since eating and drinking are among the principal diversions as well as basic necessities while traveling, you might as well take advantage of any of the specialities of the Dodecannese. The basic menu in these islands, of course, is that found throughout most of Greece (see "Food and Drink" in Practical Information A to Z) but there are some variations in the Dodecannese that visitors will want to sample.

Inevitably, fishes are among the pleasures of these islands. In particular, there is a kind of bouillabaise, or "fish stew," known as **plaki** that is sometimes found in restaurants of the Dodecannese. The islands also pride themeselves on their fine squid, or **kalamaria:** not everyone immediately takes to the idea of squid, but they are one of the pleasures of the Greek cuisine. Kos boasts of its excellent fresh fish – particularly its sinagrida, a seabream, and its **lithrini,** a small black fish. Leros boasts of its **marithes,** smelt; Kalymnos prides itself on its **ksifiyes,** swordfish, and **octopothi keftethes** – octopus meatballs! But almost any fresh fish grilled to order should prove a delight.

Try the fish with one of the local or at least Dodecannese wines. Rhodes boasts of its Lindos, a dry white, as well as of its Embona and Chevaliers de Rhodes. Kos, meanwhile, boasts of its Glafkos, its Tsirini, and its Theokritos.

Fresh fruits in season are another of the pleasures of

Two beautiful restaurants

43

Cleaning fish by the water

Fruitshop

variety of fruits that it proudly offers – figs, lemons, oranges, and pears among them.

Then there are the little unexpected treats: Kalymnos's main port, Pothia, offers a special sweet known as **Copenhai** (from Copenhagen). Leros puts caper leaves in saldas (claimed to be an aphrodisiac, if that interests you). And there will be other unfamiliar foods that appears on the menus throughout the Dodecannese. Having gone to all the trouble to come this far, you should try at least some of them.

travel throughout Greece. Kos is particularly proud of its watermelons, figs, cherries, bananas, and pomegranates; Kalymnos is proud of its tangerines, oranges, and figs; 44 Rhodes, of course, has a

3. Rhodes

AN INTRODUCTION

Writing about Greek islands can so exhaust the vocabulary of superlatives, but Rhodes surely deserves several. For Rhodes not only stands out among the Dodecannese nor even just among the islands of Greece: it stands out among all the great islands of this earth as one of those truly special places. Rhodes has been attracting foreigners at least since the Minoans came over from Crete about 1500 BC and has been inspiring poets at least since Pindar wrote his famous 7th Olympian Ode in 464 BC; wealthy Romans began to use Rhodes as a vacation resort, and by the late 19th century Rhodes was already the goal of the then elite who could afford to travel to distant and sunny islands. Today Rhodes is far more accessible to far more people but it still retains its nickname, "Island of the Sun." It also has a second nickname, Island of the Rose – some claim because its name comes from the Greek for rose, **rhodon.** (But this rose is not the familiar rose of more northern lands but the rockrose, of the genus **Cistus.**) As the pioneer of Greek tourism, Rhodes now offers perhaps the most complete spectrum of attractions to vacationers outside of Athens – including a gambling casino, a fine selection of hotels of all classes, restaurants serving a cosmopolitan selection of foods, tourist amenities of all sorts. Yet it remains in other respects an island where anyone can soon get away to little-visited corners and villages, an island of relaxation and beaches and congenial people. All of Rhode's attractions will be introduced in the following pages.

THE PHYSICAL PRESENCE

Rhodes is by far the largest of the Dodecannese, with its 1,450 square kms (540 square miles); this area is spread out on a sort of elongated diamond that is about 80 kms long and 38 kms at its widest. It is only some 11 kms (7 miles) from the coast of Turkey. Its population is about 65,000.

Rhodes is both one of the greenest, most fertile of the Dodecannese and one of the most mountainous; the whole central core of Rhodes is dominated by a series of hills and mountains, the highest peak being Mt. Atavyros at 1,215 meters (some 4,000 ft.); other notable peaks are Mt. Profitis Elias (some 800 meters) and **Mt. Acramitis** (823 meters). Rhodes has numerous springs, adequate rain during the fall-to-spring months, and supports a rich vegetation. Its forests are no longer as thick as those that once supplied wood for shipbuilders, but it has a varied range from 45 conifers to bushes and shrubs to many wild flowers and aromatic plants. There are numerous birds, some small mammals (such as hares, martens, badgers, and foxes) and deer (but these re-introduced by the Italians earlier in this century). Rhodes was once noted for its many snakes; visitors will be unlikely ever to see any – including one small poisonous species – nor are they apt to see the "Rhodes dragon," a large lizard **(Agama stellio).**

What visitors will experience are rainless, sun-filled days virtually from the first of April to the end of October, with breezes that keep the island from becoming uncomfortably hot. In short, an almost ideal paradise for vacationers.

RHODES IN MYTH AND HISTORY

Although many people come to Rhodes simply to enjoy its modern amenities and its sunshine, the island in fact can claim a very rich heritage of myth, legend, literature, and history.

There are several myths that relate the origins and early phase of the island. One such myth claims that the first inhabitants were the Telchines, amphibious creatures, human from the waist up and fish or serpents from the waist down; Poseidon was raised by them and fell in love with one of them, the nymph Halia; he

begot six sons and a daughter, Rhode, with Halia; when the six brothers insulted Aphrodite, she made them go mad and they ravished their own mother; Poseidon sank them underground; when Zeus sent a great flood, all the Telchines except Rhode left the island.

At this point, another myth takes over. Helios, son of the Titan Hyperion, was charged with driving a four-horse chariot daily across the heavenly sky, from the far east to the far west; on the day when Zeus was allotting the various cities and islands to the many gods, Helios was off doing his daily work and Zeus forgot him; on his return, Zeus apologized and said he would begin all over again, but Helios said that this was unnecessary: he had noticed a new island emerging from the sea, just off Asia Minor, and he would settle for that. Zeus assigned this new island to Helios, who soon fell in love with the nymph Rhode; she bears Helios seven sons and a daughter, and these sons rule Rhodes and become astronomers. One of these sons, Kerkaphos, fathered three sons – **Kamiros, Ialyssos,** and **Lindos** – who found the three historical cities of the island that eventually (408 BC) found a joint capital, the present city of Rhodes.

Such myths clearly reflect various fundamentals of life on Rhodes: its geological formation, rising from the sea;

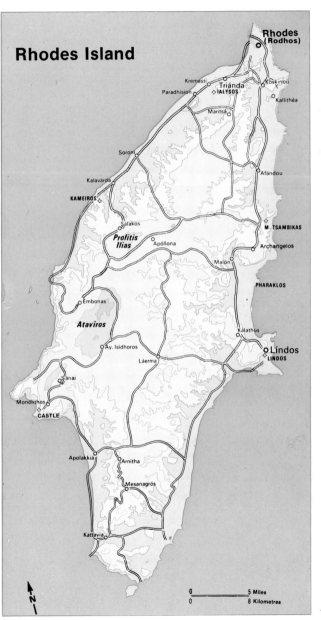

Rhodes Island

Rhodes
(Rodhos)

Kremasti Triánda Koskinoú
Paradhísion ◇IALYSOS
Kallithéa
Maritsá

Soroní

Afándou

Kalavárda

KAMEIROS ◇

Salakos
M. TSAMBIKAS ◇
Profítis
Ilías Apóllona
Archángelos
Malón

PHARAKLOS

Émbonas

Atáviros

Áy. Isídhoros Kálathos
Láerma Líndos
◇LINDOS

Sánai

Monólithos
◇CASTLE

Apolakkiá Arnítha

Mesanagrós

Kattaviá

0   5 Miles

0   8 Kilometres

47

the favor of the sun, Helios; the pre-Greek names (e.g. Kamiros, Lindos, Rhodes itself) that suggest pre-Greek inhabitants from Asia Minor. Yet another myth involves King Athaemenes, son of Katreus and grandson of Minos, king of Crete; warned by an oracle that Katreus would be killed by one of his children, Althaemenes leaves Crete and goes to Rhodes, where he founds the city of Cretenia; Althaemenes later settled at Kamiros where he raised an altar to Zeus, and around this altar he set bronze bulls that roared whenever Rhodes was threatened. Years later, the aging Katreus comes to Rhodes, but he is mistaken for a pirate and killed by a spear thrown by his own son, Althaemenes. Such a story seems to record a Minoan settlement on Rhodes.

Still a later period on Rhodes is reflected in the tale of Tiepolemos, a son of Herakles who lived at Tiryns; after he accidentally killed an uncle, the oracle at Delphi advises Tiepolemos to go to a "sea-surrounded land," which turns out to be Rhodes; Tiepolemos later leads nine ships from Rhodes to aid the Achaeans in the Trojan War, and there he fights Sarpedon, son of Zeus and king of the Lycians; both die. Tiepolemos will be considered by the Rhodians as the father of their race – and honored with the Tiepolemian Games – thus reflecting the Rhodians' Dorian-Greek heritage and their desire to be associated with the Trojan War.

The presence of Minoans between about 1550-1400 BC

Hotels in Rhodes

has been confirmed by modern archaeology – as has the existence of at least some Neolithic culture going back to about 3000 BC – and archaeology has also confirmed the presence of a strong Achaean-Mycenaean phase on Rhodes. But the real historic roots of the later Rhodians are embedded in the years after 1100 BC when Dorian Greeks begin to settle on Rhodes; apparently they came from the Argive region of the Peloponnesos, and soon they were dividing the island up among their three main cities – Lindos, Kamiros, and Ialyssos. Along with three other major Doric settlements – the island of Kos, and **Knidos** and **Halikarnassos** on the coast of Asia Minor – these three Rhodian cities formed the Doric Hexapolis ("Six-Cityd

Alliance"), which also included settlements on some of the other future Dodecannese islands (Nissyros, Kalymnos, Karpathos, and others). The religious center of this alliance was a temple of Apollo Triopios on the peninsula at Knidos.

By about 800 BC, the island of Rhodes found itself at the crossroads of what was to become the great revival of trade and colonization throughout the Easter Mediterranean – a revival that would eventually spread all across the Mediterranean. Rhodians begin to establish trade stations or colonies on adjacent islands, on the coast of Asia Minor, in Syria and Egypt, and in North Africa (where they founded Cyrene with Dorians from Thera, or Santorini); other Rhodians

went off to found colonies at Gela in Sicily, at Parthenope in Italy – later to become known as Naples – at Rhode in Spain, and on the Gymnesiae, or the Balearic Islands of Majorca and Minorca. Rhodes itself was obviously prospering through these centuries, and this is attested to by the jewelry and vases and bronze weapons that they exported and buried, and also by the coins that the three main cities began to mint (Kamiros the first, about 580 BC).

For several centuries, then, Rhodes enjoyed almost uninterrupted peace and it prospered accordingly. It was the Persians who first forced the Rhodians into the maelstrom of history; the Persians effectively subjugated Rhodes by 490 BC and forced the Rhodians to send 40 Rhodian ships to aid the Persians in the battle at Salamis in 480 BC. The Athenians, of course, defeated the Persians, but Rhodes now found itself more or less forced to join the so-called Delian Confederacy – really Athen's own empire. During the Peloponnesian Wars, Rhodians – as fellow Doric Greeks – probably sympathized with the Spartans, but it was not until the Athenians were defeated at the battle off Symi in 411 BC that the leaders of the three main Rhodian cities felt strong enough to turn against Athens.

At the same time, these leaders 'did something else: they merged or united their city-states and in 408 BC established a new capital on the northern coast. This was the city of Rhodes, and with its fine harbors and strong fortifications it soon became an important city. (It was also widely admired as an example of urban planning by Hippodamos of Miletus, the great architect and town-planner.) However, Rhodes now fell under the rule of the Spartans – in 396 BC – and in the evening ensuing decades of this century Rhodes found itself pretty much subject to whichever power asserted itself over the island – Athens, King Mausolus of Caria, the Macedonians of Philip II and then of Alexander the Great. With the death of Alexander and the breakup of his empire, Rhodes aligned itself with the Ptolemies, based in Alexandria, Egypt, and this led to one of the most epic sieges recorded in all history: between 305-4 BC, Demetrios the Besieger, a son of Antigonos of Macedon, laid siege to the city of Rhodes with some 400 ships, 40,000 troops, and some incredible siege machines. In the end, Demetrios had to give up and sign a peace treaty that left Rhodes independent. He also left behind his siege artillery, which the Rhodians sold; they used the profits to erect the Colossus, the 90-foot-high bronze statue of Helios, the sun god.

It was during the next 250 or so years that Rhodes enjoyed

its heyday of prosperity and reputation. The port became one of the major centers of trade among the Mediterranean powers, from Italy to Asia Minor, from Macedonia to North Africa; Rhodes' ships and crews were regarded as the best; the currency was accepted everywhere; and Rhodian commercial-maritime law was so respected that Augustus would adopt it some 300 years later for the whole Roman Empire (and it is still referred to today). The city of Rhodes had a population between 60,000-80,000 and many fine temples, schools, theaters, and statues (Pliny would later claim 2000). Among the best-known attractions of the city was its school of rhetoric, which many famous Romans – including Julius Caesar, Cicero, Cato, and Lucretius – would attend. So admired was Rhodes that when a great earthquake ruined much of the

city in 227 BC – bringing down the Colossus – rulers and city-states and individuals all over the Mediterranean contributed to its reconstruction. Although the Colossus lay there, Rhodes was soon rebuilt.

Through these many years, however, Rhodes became increasingly subject to the newly emerging power to its west – Rome. Rhodes aligned itself with Rome at times and was rewarded with control over various territory and islands in the eastern Mediterranean, but there was never any real doubt as to where the real power was. Rhodes eventually got caught between the factions in the Romans' civil wars, and after the assassination of Julius Caesar in 44 BC, Cassius fled and then laid siege to Rhodes; taking the city in 43 BC, he plundered it, killed many citizens, and pretty much wiped out the Rhodian fleet. Rhodes never really

Governor's house

The Entrance to the harbour at night   and during the day

recovered as a naval power, and although Augustus would extend the title of "Allied City," Vespasian had simply absorbed Rhodes into the Roman Empire by AD 79.

During the next 1,200 years, Rhodes was essentially subject to whatever natural and human forces moved across its path. Romans, Goths, Byzantines, Persians, Saracens, Seljuks – all had their day on Rhodes. So, too, did several devastating earthquakes. The only saving grace during these long dark centuries was the coming of Christianity: St. Paul the Apostle put in at Rhodes (by legend, at Lindos) in AD 57, soon there was a Christian community, before long a bishop of Rhodes was the Metropolitan seat of the whole region. The Crusaders

Fountain

Kiosque

from Western Europe eventually passed through, and when the Fourth Crusade set up their own empire in Constantinople, the Greek governor of Rhodes, Leon Gavalas, proclaimed Rhodes independent. But Rhodes soon reverted to the Byzantine Empire, although its actual rulers were often Italians from Genoa. It was one of these, Vignolo Vignoli, who in 1306 made the way clear for the Knights of St. John of Jerusalem – and Rhode's next great historical phase.

The Knights of St. John of 53

West Coast beach: The City of Rhodes in the background

Jerusalem had grown out of a hospital established in Jerusalem in 1058 by Italian monks to help pilgrims in the Holy Land; gradually the military arm attracted young noblemen from Western Europe who were mainly interested in fighting the "infidels"; eventually these knights were driven from Palestine and took refuge in Cyprus in 1291; their search for a permanent home led them to Rhodes, and in 1306 Vignoli sold them a part of Rhodes (along with the islands of Kos and Leros; by 1309, the Knights simply took over the city and the island. For over two centuries the Knights dominated Rhodes while fighting against the

Moslems throughout the eastern Mediterranean. They did succeed in reviving Rhodes' economy and commercial relations, but they were also subject to three sieges from Moslems, falling to the last of these, on December 29, 1522. This siege was one of the most spectacular of such events throughout all history; Suleiman II the Magnificent personally led its final phase, which involved 300 ships, 1000 cannon and about 100,000 troops arrayed against only about 6000 defenders inside the great walls of Rhodes. The last Grand Master of the Knights,

The street of the Kinghts

Another view of the City of Rhodes

Villiers de l'Isle Adam, left Rhodes on January 1, 1523 with the 180 surviving knights and went to Crete, finally settling on Malta in 1530.

Now Rhodes found itself under yet another foreign power, the Turks, and for almost four centuries life there became if not necessarily grim, at least unstimulating. Then in 1912, after a brief war that Italy had instigated simply to seize territory from a weakening Ottoman Turkish Empire, Rhodes and the other Dodecannese were taken over by the Italians. At first the islands' inhabitants thought they were to be turned free to be Greeks once more, but the Italians stayed on; the second Treaty of Lausanne in 1923 gave the Dodecannese to Italy. During World War II, British and other Allied forces gradually liberated the islands in 1944-45. Finally, after over 2000 years of foreign occupation or interference, Rhodes and the

other Dodecannese formally were united with the rest of Greece on October 28, 1947.

In the decades since 1947, Rhodes has undergone yet another of its "renaissances" as measured by economic prosperity and international contacts – in this case, largely generated by foreign tourists. With its charter flights and tour groups, discos and boutiques, casino and luxury hotels, Rhodes is obviously in danger of losing some of its indigenous character. But since it has survived all these centuries as a "crossroads" culture, it probably will somehow emerge intact from even the 20th century.

TRAVELING TO AND ON RHODES

Ships and airplanes to Rhodes It should be clear from the general discussion of the means of getting to the Dodecannese – see pp.   – that

Fishing boats

Rhodes is by far the most accessible of these islands. It is in fact the hub of the air routes and many of the ship lines. The one point that should be re-emphasized here is that Rhodes is linked to both Crete and to the Eastern Sporades (via Patmos and **Samos**) and thus may be included in combination with almost any other Aegean island.

Getting around Rhodes: Although you can walk around the city of Rhodes and see its many attractions, if you want to see Lindos or any of the other sites and attractions on the island you will have to find some sort of transportation. There is public bus service to most all of the places and locales most people would be interested in viewing; schedules to and from Lindos especially allow for a convenient one-day excursion, with plenty of time to see the ancient remains, the medieval town,

and even to enjoy the nearby beach and eating places. A few of the more remote beaches or points of interest might involve a short walk from the bus stops. There are also tour buses that operate out of the city of Rhodes – not to mention the more expensive tours that originate in Athens and involve flights to Rhodes, hotels, meals, buses, and all. There are cars, motorbikes, and bicycles to rent; there are taxis that a group of 3–5 might find even more convenient than buses or car rental; and there are boats that take groups on day excursions to beaches around the island. Whatever your tastes or budget, you will have no trouble traveling around Rhodes.

ACCOMMODATIONS ON RHODES

Hotels: There must be at least 200 hotels on Rhodes just in the Luxury, Class A, B, and 57

C categories, not to mention countless more less ambitious hotels and rooms to rent. These latter tend to be located in the Old Town of Rhodes; usually they involve sharing a toilet and bath; if not to everyone's taste, they at least remind you that you're not visiting some timeless international resort. And be warned: if you arrive on Rhodes during the peak months, you may have little choice – at least in the city of Rhodes and in the middle price-range. If there is any question, go to the Tourist Office or Tourist Police in the New Town, corner of Papagos and Makarios Streets; even in the most crowded times, they can find you a room in someone's house. Don't forget, either, that there is a fair selection of hotels elsewhere around the island – especially at the beach at **Faliraki.**

Restaurants: As with the hotels, the city of Rhodes offers a tremendous selection, from a fish taverna (Manolis) that some experienced travelers regard as among the best such in all of Greece to places that serve undistinguished meals to unsuspecting tourists. Be aware that on in the evening some places introduce music – and the cost of drinks may rise considerably. In the city of Rhodes, keep your eyes

Two of the most famous hotels on the island of Rhodes

open to possibilities as you walk around during the day – checks out menus and prices and decor. Expensive places are usually unapologetically so; tourist traps are usually blatantly so. But don't forget that the city of Rhodes is geared to international and mass tourism; you might prefer to wander away from the main streets and try some less fashionable places.

ACTIVITIES AND DIVERSIONS

Some will go to Rhodes strictly for the archaeological and historical remains, while others will head straight for the beach. But between these two extremes lie many other possibilities for enlivening your stay on Rhodes.

Swimming & Water-sports: Rhodes boasts of several fine beaches: Faliraki (quite developed), Safikos Beach, Prassonisi, Kolimbia (at Seven Springs), the beach below Lindos, the Bay of Ladiko. The larger hotels offer water-skiing; sail-surfboards and paddle boats may be rented; snorkeling is always a possibility.

Golf & Tennis: There is an 18-hole golf course near the city of Rhodes and there are

A restaurant at night

tennis courts – all open to the public: inquire at the Tourist Office if you want to pursue either.

Mountaineering: There are numerous peaks and trails that can be tried by those with at least some experience; the only marked trail is that leading from the village of Empona to the top of Mt. Atavyros.

Fishing & Hunting: The best fishing is reputed to be off the shores of Lindos, Kamiros, **Kallithea,** and **Gennadi.** No license is required. However, a license would be required for hunting: the game would be hare, partridge, dove, quail, and wild duck; near Gennadi village, snipe are taken.

Music & Dance: Perhaps the best way to experience authentic Greek music and dance, on Rhodes as elsewhere, is to attend a wedding or nameday celebration or just to drop in a local cafe or celebrations. There are several restaurants in the city of Rhodes that feature ·quite authentic folk dancing – the Spilia in the Old Town and the Nor (on Mandraki Harbor) being among the best known. If you enjoy a full performance of folk dancing by trained dancers, the Nelly Dimoglou Folk Dance Troupe, one of the oldest such in Greece, performs in the city of Rhodes from June to October.

Sound & Light: Otherwise

known as Son et Lumière (because it originated in France) this offers an evening production that focuses on the Grand Master's Palace and recounts the history of medieval Rhodes as it revolved around the Knights of St. John of Jerusalem. These performances are given several nights a week – taking turns in various languages – from April to October, if you've never attended one of these productions, here's a chance to learn a bit of history under the stars.

Wine Festival: One of the oldest and most popular of the several now held around Greece, this is held at Rodini, on the edge of the city of Rhodes, between July and September. Lots of good, cheap wine and food.

Casino: Not everyone's need when visiting Rhodes, but it certainly appeals to many, who gamble away the nights from 7pm to 4am; roulette, chemin-de-fer, blackjack, and slot machines are offered. It is located in the luxury class Grand Hotel Astir Palace. There is a modest entrance fee and a modest minimum. After that, you're on your own.

Tourists using "Local Transportation"

"International" restaurant

4. The City of Rhodes

The city is practically divided into two parts, the Old Town and New Town; although the passenger ships deposit visitors at the central, or commercial, port below the **Old Town,** the buses from the airport leave arrivals in the **New Town;** in any case, since visitors spend a fair amount of time in this New Town, let us describe it first.

Its focal point is its harbor, known as **Mandraki,** which is actually the Greek word for a sheepfold; instead of enclosing sheep this lovely harbor now is crowded with yachts from all over the world and smaller fishing and excursion boats. During the rule of the Knights, shipwrights practiced their craft here (which may account for another occasional name, Harbor of the Galleys). But there had always been some harbor about here, and it is now generally agreed that it was at the entrance to this harbor that the Colossus of Rhodes stood. As mentioned in the history (p. 50), this statue was paid for by the sale of the siege machines left behind by Demetrios Poliorketes ("The Besieger") in 304 BC; it is attributed to the sculptor Chares, from Lindos, and was made of bronze; standing some 120 feet high, it represented **Helios,** the sun god and protector of Rhodes, holding a torch in his right hand – presumably lit at night to serve as a beacon. What the Colossus did not do was to "bestride" the harbor, as so often depicted, for ships to pass under. Erected about 29(

BC, it was so extraordinary that it made the list of Seven Wonders of the Ancient World, yet by 225BC it fell in an earthquake and lay there for almost 800 years; the superstitious people of that age did not steal the valuable bronze, but in AD 653 Saracen Arabs carried off the fragments and sold them in Tyre to merchants who supposedly carried the bronze off on 900 camels and then melted it down.

Now the Mandraki is guarded by two bronze statues of deer (for which Rhodes was long famous); there are modern (and the outer one replaces a statue of the Roman she-wolf that the Italians had erected). The mole, or breakwater, that runs along the east side is marked by three old windmills, and at its end is the towerfort of **St. Nicholas,** built in 1464-67 by the Grand Master Zacosta; it now serves as a lighthouse.

The Mandraki shoreline is a long, lively esplanade, anchored at its south end by the Nea Agora, or **New Market,** a large many-sided structure in a pseudo-Turkish style; it is filled with shops and cafes lining both its exterior and the interior courtyard, and sitting at one of these cafes for a while is a perfect way to observe the passing scene in Rhodes. In the streets that extend beyond and behind the Nea Agora is the modern commercial center of Rhodes, the offices of the National Tourist Organization and the Tourist Police, the banks, and numerous hotels.

Proceeding north along the Mandraki esplande, you come across a series of suspiciously Italian looking structures; indeed they, were erected between 1912-1940 when the Italians were ruling Rhodes, and they are principally designed by Florestano di Fausto. The Law Courts is the first building, on your left, and at the edge of the harbor, facing this, is the **Cathedral,** or Church of the Evangelist, erected in 1925; on its west side is a fountain that is a copy of the 13th-century Fontana Grande at Viterbo, Italy. Extending behind the cathedral is the Nomarkhia, or Prefect's Office (the Governor's Palace under the Italians), in a Venetian-Gothic style. Facing the square are the Post Office, the City Hall, and the **Municipal Theater.**

Behind this theater is the **Mosque of Murad Reis,** with its elegant minaret; Murad Reis was the admiral of the Turkish fleet during the great siege of 1522, and his tomb is in the circular structure in front of the mosque; the Moslem cemetery alongside the mosque holds the tombs of various Turks who died in exile on Rhodes. Proceeding still farther northwards and passing various fine hotels, you come out to the northernmost tip of the city and the entire island; here is located the Hydrobio- 63

A view of Mandraki. The Palace of the Grand Master in the background

logical Institute, which has displays of unusual preserved marine life, and an Aquarium, which although hardly of world class is still of interest with its coral-lined tanks.

Before plunging into the Old Town, it might be advisable to seek out the Acropolis of the ancient city; it is located about a 20-minute walk due west of the Old Town, and since the monuments themselves are not all that important or exciting, a visit at sunset is perhaps the best way to reward your exertions. The ancient city seems to have extended along this west shore, from the Acropolis to the northern tip, and many remains of walls,

streets, and houses are found throughout this area. The Acropolis itself is now known as Mt Ayios Stefanos by Greeks, but as Mt. Smith by the international community: this comes from British Admiral Sir Sidney Smith who in 1802 lived in a house here to observe the movements of the French fleet.

If you have made your way along Diagoridon Street, down to the left in a grove of olives, is the Stadium (greatly restored by the Italians) dating from the 2nd century BC; a small, almost square amphitheater (with only three seats and the orchestra from the original); west of the theater is a large

retaining wall for an upper terrace, on which stand some remains of the **Temple of Pythian Apollo** (only fragments of the original). Farther north along the ridge was the Temple of Zeus and another dedicated to Athena Polias (with a few remains of each). Tombs of the Hellenistic period are located south of the Acropolis. Again, nothing all that exciting, but the walk and the view provide a refreshing intermission from all the crowds in the Old Town.

RHODES; OLD TOWN

Coming from the New Town, most people will enter the Old Town through the New Gate, or **Gate of Liberty** opened through the old walls in 1924): off to the side are the gardens where you sit below the medieval walls to watch the Sound and Light show. You are now in the part of the Old Town traditionally known as the **Collachium:** this is where the Knights themselves lived and governed, while the rest of the Old Town was inhabited by the Greeks, Jews, and other Mediterraneans who had been drawn to Rhodes. You come into **Arsenal Square,** or Plateia Symi; Arsenal Gate leads out to the commercial harbor; here are remains of the 3rd-century BC Temple of Aphro- 65

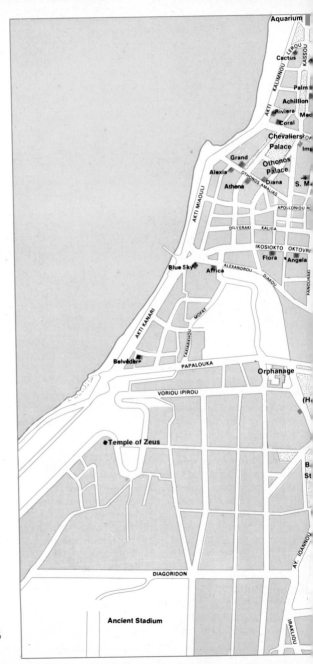

Aquarium

Cactus

Palm

Achillion

Riviera

Coral

Med

Chevaliers
Palace

Grand

Othonos
Palace

Alexis

Athena

Diana

S. M

APOLLONIOU RO

DILVERAKI

KALIGA

IKOSIOKTO OKTOVRI

Flora

Angela

Blue Sky

Africa

ALEXANDROU

DIAKOU

MOFAT

TAXIARKHOU

Belvedere

PAPALOUKA

Orphanage

VORIOU IPIROU

(H

Temple of Zeus

B
St

DIAGORIDON

Ancient Stadium

AKTI KALIMNOU

LEROU

KASSOU

AKTI

OTHONOS AMALIAS

AKTI MIAOULI

FANDURAKI

AKTI KANARI

AV. IOANNOU

IRAKLIOU

Rhodes

0   400 Meters
0   400 Yards

SAVA

PLAT
KOUNDOURIOTOU

Mosque

Nat. Th.

Nomarchia

PLAT
VAS YEORYIOU II

Dimarchion

Cathedral

PLAT
ELEVTHERIAS

ou LOKHOU

THELONTIONTNS

Law courts

ARTIOU

Kamiros

NTO

egina

MAKARIOU

Spartalis

GALLIAS

ni

AGOU

St. Nicholas

AKTI BOUBOULI

Three Windmills

Bastion of St. Paul

Tower of St. Peter

New Gate

Tower of Naillac (site)

St Demetrios

Classical excavation

Temple

Arsenal Gate

Palace of
3d. Masters

Garden

Palace

Inn of Auvergne

Custom house

IPPOTON

St. Mary's

Port

sh sch.

Hospital
(Mus.)

Arnaldo Gate

maly

Suleymaniye
Cami

SOKRATOUS

Chadravan
Cami

Agha
Cami

ERMOU

Castellania

Our Lady of Victory

kaci
ni

Mustapha
Cami

AY. FANOURIOU

Fountain

Ibrahim Pacha
Cami

ARISTOTELOUS

Admirally

PINDAROU

St
Pantaleon
Hosp.

Bey

Hamam

Demirli
Cami

Our Lady

ICHADEF

St. Catherine

Kavakly
Mescidi

of the City

dul Celil
Mescidi

Cami

PITHAGORA

PERIKLEOUS

OMIROU

Bab
Mestud
Cami

Borouzan
Mescidi

Dolaply
Mescidi

Ilk Mihrab
Cami

IRINIS

IRODOTOU

EFTHIMIOU

Bastion of Carretto

St. Athanasius Gate

VIRONOS

KANADA

St. Francis R.C.

Koskinou Bastion
and Gate

Stadium

A view of Mandraki from the Palace of the Grand Master

dite, a Byzantine fountain, and heaps of cannonballs (said to have been collected during the siege of 1522). Behind the ancient temple remains is the Inn of **Tongue of Auvergne** (from the 15th century, but restored in 1919): the reason for "The Tongue" will be discussed below.

In the square opposite the Inn of Auvergne is the Palace of the Armeria, built in the 14th century by a Grand Master Roger de Pinsot; it served as the first hospital of the Knights, and now houses the Institute of History and Archaeology and the Ephorate

of Antiquities; also located here is the Museum of Popular Decorative Arts (open only for a few hours on selected days of the week: inquite as soon as you arrive in Rhodes if you are especially interested in such collections).

Proceeding under an archway through a small passageway behind the Inn of Auvergne, you will come to find on your left, the 13th-century Orthodox church of St. Mary the Roman Catholic Knights used it for their cathedral, and then the Turks converted into a mosque, the Enderoum Tzami; it is now a museum

Byzantine work, primarily liturgical objects.

Diagonally opposite this church and on the corner of the famed Street of the Knights – which we shall explore shortly – is a massive building, the **Hospital of the Knights,** begun in 1440 and completed by 1489; it was restored under the Italians after the Turks had allowed it to deteriorate by using it as a barracks; the original cypress door was given to Louis-Philippe of France in 1836 by the Sultan Mahmoud and it can still be seen at Versailles. Seven of the arches lead to storage areas, or magazines, while the eighth serves as the gateway, which leads into the Great Court, enclosed by a double portico. The ground floor served as storage and service areas for the hospital, which occupied the upper story, which you go up to by an outside stairway on the left. The main ward of the hospital occupied the long hall along the front; it is divided into two aisles by seven pillars; the arches of the arcade support a sloping roof of cypress; this ward was designed for 32 beds (although it could hold far more in an emergency). An arch in the wall opposite the entrance leads into a small chapel, where mass was said daily. (You are now standing over the main gateway.) The refectory and kitchen of the hospital were in the rooms to the right (or south) of the ward.

The Hospital of the Knights now houses the Archaeological Museum (with a modest admission fee, and standard Greek visiting hours). It is well worth at least a short visit by

Liberty Gate

The Entrance to the Palace of the Grand Master

those with any interest in ancient Rhodes. Its exhibits range from the Mycenaean age through the Hellenistic, and include objects not only from sites on Rhodes but also from several other islands of the Dodecannese. The two most admired objects are a statuette known as **Aphrodite of Rhodes,** a kneeling maiden separating her hair as she emerges from the sea (1st c.BC); and the **Aphrodite Thalassia,** or Venus Pudica (Chaste), a marble statue found in the sea off Rhodes (3rd c. BC).

Outside the Hospital-Museum, to the left is Street of the Knights; the cobbled street and its handsome buildings have been meticulously restored to become an almost "pure" medieval street, but there is something rather sterile and lifeless about it.

Still, it's a place you must visit. This was the main street of the Collachium, and several of the "Tongues" had their Inns, or headquarters here. The Order of the Knights of St. John of Jerusalem was divided originally into seven groups based on their national homelands in Europe -- and thus called "Tongues": **Provence, Auvergne, France, Italy, England, Germany,** and **Spain** (which was later divided into the separate "tongues" of **Aragon** and **Castille**). Each Tongue elected its own leader and these leaders formed the **Council of the Order,** which in turn elected the **Grand Master** who served for life; between 1309 and 1522, there were 19 Grand Masters, and they

Rhodes by night: The Government House (top) and the Palace of the Grand Master.

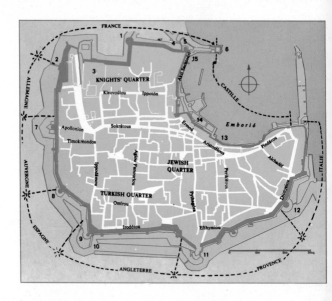

1. Tower of St. Peter
2. Gate of Amboise
3. Palace of Gd. Masters
4. New Gate
5. Bastion of St. Paul
6. Tower of Naillac
7. Bastion of George
8. Tower of Spain

9. Tower of St. Mary
10. Gate of St. Athanasius
11. Koskinou Bastion and Gate
12. Bastion of Carretto
13. Castellania
14. Marine Gate
15. Arsenal Gate

Plan of the Old City

effectively ruled Rhodes as well as their Order. The Order itself was made up of three classes of men: the Knights who were both warriors and administrators (and were often younger sons of European aristocracy); the Catholic priests; and "serving brothers," who performed the supporting operations.

Along the street, then, you will note the Inns of several of the Tongues -- that of Italy,

France, Spain, and Provence -- with numerous architectural elements and coats of arms, the Chapel of the Tongue of France is also notable.

You come out at the end of the street into the Citadel, or **St. John's Church,** Square (The loggia is a modern reconstruction.) On the left once stood the Chruch of St John, which contained the tombs of certain Knights; the Turks turned it into a mosque but it was destroyed in 1856 when lightning struck the minaret and exploded a long-ago buried store of gunpowder (and killing several hundred people).

Dominating the square, as it does the whole Collachium, is the Palace of the Grand Masters. On the site of an ancient temple to Apollo, the Knights quickly set to work to erect, a massive palace-fortress, which they had finished by the end of the 14th century. It was the residence of the Grand Master and the main assembly for the Order, and with its extensive storerooms it could withstand a siege. Under the Turks, who used it as a prison, it deteriorated and earthquakes (and the lightning-explosion of 1856) further

The Remains from the Temple of Apollo on the Acropolis of Rhodes

Another view of the palace of the Grand Master

damaged it. The Italians in this century restored the exterior in the original manner, but redid the interior in a mixture of styles, using everything from Renaissance woodwork (from Italy) and ancient mosaics from the island of Kos. It was intended to serve as a summer palace for King Victor Emmanuel III and then for Mussolini. Most visitors today find it incongruous if not downright tasteless, but it might be worth a quick look-around.

Leaving the **Palace of the Grand Masters,** you may proceed out of the right (west) end of the square through the **Artillery Gate** to emerge onto a pleasant square lined with shops and cafes and shade-trees. As its far (north) end is the **Amboise Gate** that leads out across the moat and the old walls to the New Town. But you will most likely want to turn south and pass along the **Clock Tower,** a modern eyesore (replacing a 15th century tower) to proceed into **Suleiman Square.** Dominating it is **Suleiman's Mosque,** originally built here in 1522 but pretty much rebuilt in 1808; it has a fountain in its forecourt and an especially elegant minaret. Opposite the mosque is

74

the **Ahmed Hafouz Library,** or Turkish Library, dating from the 18th century but with an illuminated Koran of the 14th-15th centuries.

From Suleiman Square, you could choose to go off in one of two main expeditions; sooner or later, you'll want to explore both parts of the Old City. One expedition takes you into the old Turkish quarter, with its several mosques and other institutions plus a warren of medieval streets and houses. This old Turkish quarter lies essentially south of Suleiman Square, although one notable building is on the street to the right, **Othos Apollonion;** halfway or so toward the outer wall, on the right, is the **Khurmale Medresses,** "College

The Mosque of Murad Reis

The Archaeological Museum

of the Date-Palm," as the Turks named the building that they adapted from an old Greek Orthodox church of the 14th century; its dome retains some of the original tiles.

If you have at least an hour or two plus the interest to wander through an almost medieval quarter, you should explore this section of Old Rhodes. It is rather rundown, most of the mosques are abandoned, there is nothing all that spectacular; but it is perfectly safe and will reward

Nike of Samothrace

Laocoon Group

A Carved Ship in relief on a rock on the Acropolis of Lindos

Statues of Nymphs

all those with an eye for the wayward and serendipitous pleasures of traveling. The area involved is only about 10 acres altogether, so it's not a question of long distances. But the streets and alleys wind here and there, and you'll want to allow time for peeking and poking around. (Remember, though, that people live in these houses and streets and expect to be respected, not regarded as museum displays).

Most of the mosques date from the 15th and 16 centuries, but were of often built upon earlier Christian churches.

Back at **Suleiman Square,** most visitors will probably first take the other route out: due east along **Socrates Street,** the main shopping street of the city, at least for foreigners. It really has a bazaar atmosphere -- yes, and bizarre, too, in its juxtaposition of gaudy commercialism with some traditio-

The three Windmills of Rhodes

A view of the town

Over the Entrance to the Palace of the Grand Master

The Admiral's Gate

The Mosque of Suleiman

nal and indigenous elements. Everyone who comes to Rhodes has to walk along it at least once, whether you buy anything or not. Expensive fur and jewelry stores sit smack alongside cheap souvenir and snack shops, and this is what makes the experience so diverting.

On the way down the street, you'll pass, right, the **Mosque of Aga,** sitting on pillars; and then come down into **Hippocrates Square** with its fountain. The square is dominated by the **Palace** of the **Castellan,** dating from 1507. It is believed to have served as either (or both) the commercial court of the Knights or as a merchants' meeting hall; the Turks turned the upper story into a mosque and the ground floor into a

The Amboise Gate

fish market. You can visit the upper hall by ascending the exterior stairway and passing through a sculptured stone doorway.

Off to the left is the impressive **Marine Gate,** which gives passage through the medieval walls to the commericl port (while still farther right, or north, along the old walls is the equally impressive **Arnaldo Gate**). If you go out through the Marine Gate, at least for a moment, you can see the large commercial harbor, enclosed by two moles; the one to the north (left) was once incorporated into the city's walls, and was domianted at the end by the **Tower of Naillac** (so named from the Knights' Grand Master between 1396-1421, Philibert de Naillac); it was destroyed in the earthquake of 1863 (although there has been talk of reconstructing it). The other, larger mole, to the right, is where the main ships now tie up and it's now dominated by the customs house.

Back inside the **Marine Gate** and don't neglect to look up at its various bas-reliefs and escutcheons -- you continue past the **Palace of the Castellan** and onto Aristotle Street, which leads into **Martyrs' Square,** dominated by the Archbishop's Palace; dating from the 15th century, it has also come to be known as "The Admiralty," but it seems to have been the residence of either an Orthodox or Roman Catholic Archbishop, judging from inscriptions still there. Still continuing along the edge of the old city, you come onto **Pindar Street;** this crosses a street that leads through an opening in the old wall, and on your right you will see the apse of the Church of St. Mary of the City (or Our Lady of the Bourg); dating from the early 15th century, this Roman Catholic church must have been quite an impressive Gothic structure.

Pindar Street (Othos Pindarou) continues on past the **Hospice of St. Catherine,** right, established in the late 14the century to aid Italian pilgrims to the Holy Land (then enlarged in the early 16th century). At the far end of the old city, on the ramparts, there once stood a church, **Our Lady of Victory,** built by the Knights to honour a successful

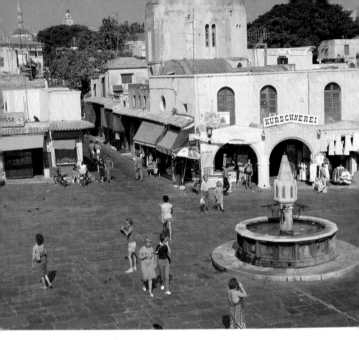

Ippocrates square

The Square of the Jewish Martyrs

defense in 1480 but then destroyed shortly after the Turks triumphed in 1522. The gate onto the harbor here is known as St. Catherine's.

THE MEDIEVAL WALLS OF RHODES

Even if you are not particularly knowledgeable about or addicted to medieval fortifications you cannot help but be impressed by the great walls of Rhodes; certainly they rank among the half dozen such construction feats now surviving in the world. Their total circumference is about 2 1/2 miles, but you need not walk the entire length to get a sense of the achievement. There are tours at least a couple days a week traditionally setting out from the Palace of the Grand Masters in the late afternoon: inquire at the National Tourist Organization office as soon as you arrive but there are numerous points of entry as you make your way around the Old City, and you should at least walk a stretch of the parapet.

There was some walled fortification here during the Byzantine era, but it was unable to hold off the Knights for more than about three years. Little remains from those Byzantine walls, because successive generations of the Knights made such extensive additions starting in the early 14th century and up to the final siege in 1522. The end

A view of the Entrance to the Palace of the Grand Master

result is truly monumental beyond any Hollywood epic fantasy: a wall that rises from a moat (that was never filled with water) and is topped by a broad walk, with numerous battlements, embrasures, and towers or bastions. At some places there is a second and outer wall, technically known as the circumvallation.

In 1465, the ramparts were divided into eight sectors, or bulwarks, each the responsibility of one of the "Tongues"; this must have reflected the internal "blocs" of the Knights, but it must also have proven efficient in battles, when the men needed to communicate quickly with fellow defenders. The French Ton-gue were responsible for the entire north side – from the **Tower of Naillac** at the harbor's edge, along the outside of the **Palace of the Grand Masters** and around onto the northwest corner to the **Amboise Gate;** from the **Amboise Gate** to the **St George's Tower** was the bulwark of the Tongue of Germany; from **St George's Tower** to the **Spanish Tower** was the Tongue of Auvergne; then on to the **Tower of St. Mary** was the bulwark of the Tongue of Spain (or Aragon); then the stretch along the south from **St. Mary's Tower** to **St. John's (or Koskinou) Gate** was the responsibility of the Tongue of England; the remaining stretch along the south to the **Italian Tower belonged** to the Tongue of

Reconstructed Theater on the Acropolis of Rhodes

Provence; from the **Italian (or del Caretto's) Tower** to **St. Catherine's Gate** at the south-eastern corner of the harbor belonged to the Tongue of Italy; and the long stretch around the harbor to the **Tower of Naillac** was the responsibility of the Tongue of Castile. Incidentally, the Turks were able to capture the city in December 1522 after making a final breach in the sector under the Tongue of Spain (or Aragon).

WRAPPING UP YOUR VISIT TO THE CITY OF RHODES

So this is the city of Rhodes as most visitors will choose to experience it. There's more to it – many more mosques and churches, for instance – but that requires a more specialized guide. Some people will find the city disturbingly "touristified," and there's no denying that it has been turned into something of a mecca for holidayers. But it's just as true that you are free to wander off by yourself, away from the

The Tower of Naillac

your places and the times of day, and you can be virtually alone, even at the height of the tourist season. There's always a cafe that isn't frequented by foreigners, a shop that hasn't been discovered by souvenir-hunters, a restaurant too modest to attract the international set. Above all, the city of Rhodes is made for walking through and around and in and about. (Most visitors forget to go outside the great medieval ramparts and view them from a short distance: they're at least as imposing as seen up close and inside.) So if you go to the city of Rhodes prepared to enjoy it for what it is, you'll not be disappointed.

most frequented streets and locales, and discover a quite extraordinary city. Choose

Giftshop

Shopping at Lindos

Homemade Carpets

Ceramics

Making baskets

Typical houses on the island of Rhodes

5. Lindos

This is undoubtedly the principal destination after the city of Rhodes – indeed, for those primarily interested in classical archaeology, **Lindos,** is the main attraction of the island. The classical remains certainly live up to their reputation, and their setting – high above the sea – tends to convert even those not overly impressed by marble. But a visit to Lindos holds out far more surprises and rewards, even for those who have done their homework on classical sites.

Most people will be visiting Lindos for one day only, and the public bus schedule from the new city of Rhodes allows for just such an excursion – leaving at convenient hours of the morning for Lindos and then returning at convenient hours. Many people, however, choose to go with one of the several tourist agency tours, which are probably even more convenient (and relieve you of any worry about getting a seat on the bus). Inquire and make your plans. With a climb to the acropolis, a stroll through the medieval town, and lunch, you'll want about 4 hours; more extended viewing and a swim at the beach can easily fill a day at Lindos.

THE DRIVE TO LINDOS

Most people will not be driving in their own or rented cars so they will not be able to make any stops or sidetrips on their visit to Lindos, but here are described the points of interest enroute. You might want to make a special visit to one or more of them during your stay on Rhodes.

Just about two miles after leaving the center of Rhodes, you pass through the suburb of **Rhodini,** where the annual wine festival is held between July and September. There is a lovely park here, with peacocks running about; it is claimed (although with no real evidence) that this was the location of the famed 4th-century-BC **School of Rhetoric of Aeschines,** later attended by such notable Romans as Cicero and Julius Caesar.

At about 5 miles, you pass through the village of **Koskinou:** it is known for having many houses with interior floors and courtyards laid with pebbles (a Rhodian tradition seen at its fullest in the village of Lindos). The atmosphere along this stretch is almost African.

At some 8 miles, you pass above the beach-resort of **Faliraki;** it boasts a fine sandy beach and there are several good hotels and restaurants, so Faliraki could become your homebase while on Rhodes. At about 13 miles, you pass through **Afandou,** noted for

Acropolis of Lindos with the remains of the Temple of Athena

both its handmade rugs and for the only 18-hole golf course on Rhodes; also on the road to the sea is the picturesque church of **Panayia Katholiki** (with some classical elements incorporated in its structure). Beyond the village of **Kolymvia,** at about 16 1/2 miles, a turnoff to the right would lead to **Epta Pighes** ("seven springs"), where springs form a small lake surrounded by trees. (There has been a restaurant here during the summer season.)

The road now goes through a pass, with Mt. Tsambika on the left; the monastery nearby has a fine carved ikonostasis.

You then come down into the village of **Arkhangelos;** it has a medieval castle and the 14th-century church of Ayii Theodori with frescoes, but it is known today for its locally made rugs and ceramics. The road continues through (at 24 miles) **Malona;** a turnoff to the left leads towards a promontory above the sea and the Castle of Pharaklos, built by the Knights of St. John. On the beach below, at **Haraki,** are tavernas. Passing through the village of **Kalathos,** the road then forks; that to the right leads on to the southern part of Rhodes, so we bear left and come (at about 34 miles) into

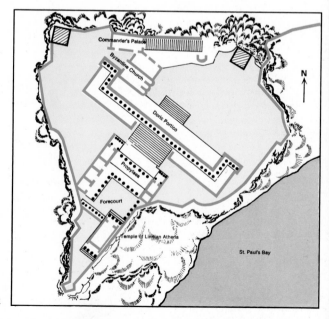

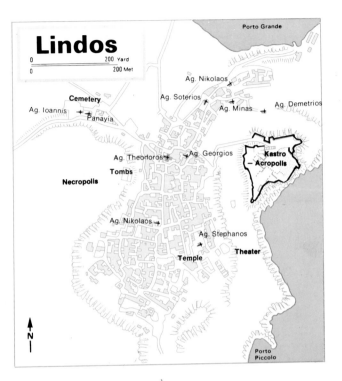

view of the village and acropolis of Lindos before pulling up at the parking area on the edge of the village. There are restaurants and cafes here, a refreshing fountain, and the road down to the beach (with still more restaurants and cafes).

Lindos boasts a history as distinguished as that of the city of Rhodes. It was settled as early as 2500 BC and by about 1000 BC there was a temple to Athena on the site. When the Dorian Greeks moved onto Rhodes, Lindos along with

Kameiros and Ialysos became the major city, thanks in part to its adjacent harbors; its citizens founded colonies at Parthenopea, which developed into Naples, Italy, and at Gela, Sicily. After the three Rhodian cities cooperated to establish Rhodes in 408 BC, Lindos lost its importance as a commercial center but it remained a religious and cultural center. Thus it was in the small bay below Lindos that St. Paul is said to have landed (about AD 60) enroute to Rome. During the long Byzantine era, the 93

The bell tower of Kimissis of Theotokou: Lindos

A house in Lindos

Acropolis of Lindos   *The harbour of St. Paul, south of Lindos*

The Entrance to the Acropolis of Lindos

acropolis served as a fortress, and it was inevitable that the Knights of St John could make it into one of their main outposts. It remained for Danish archaeologists to start the excavations of the classical remains early in the 20th century, although it was the Italians who did most of the restoration work.

Meanwhile, the village at the foot of the acropolis had become under the Knights a prosperous center; so much of this medieval Lindos survives that it has been declared a national landmark, there are no vehicles allowed on its narrow streets, and little or no changes can be made in its

Eastern part of the Doric stoa on Acropolis

buildings. Many houses survive from as far back as the 15th century; their architecture combines Gothic (from the European Knights), Byzantine Greek, and Middle Eastern elements; some have painted ceilings, and many have the distinctive white-and-black pebble floors; most ˙ extraordinary, however, are the facades, doorways, and windows with their elaborate carvings. If you are interested in such details, ask after the houses of Moschorides and Krekas; everyone should at least seek out the **House of Papas Konstandinos,** with the most ambitious architecture and carvings. There are also several medieval churches in the village; perhaps the most interesting as well as most accessible – for it is near the parking-lot square – is the church of the **Panayia,** dating from the 15th century; its frescoes, however, date from 1779.

Lindos was once known for its lace but even more so for a particular style of pottery, the so-called Lindos Ware, distinguished by its floral decorations in red on a green background. It now appears that the medieval Lindos Ware was actually made in Asia Minor, but in more recent times Rhodes has taken to making quite handsome reproductions. What is less

A view of the Doric Stoa on the Acropolis 99

Reconstruction of Acropolis of Lindos by E Dyggre

attractive to many visitors to Lindos, however, is the sheer number of souvenir shops that fill the streets enroute to the acropolis; even more appalling are the souvenirs that now spill onto the ground lining the steps and path up to the acropolis. All you can do if you're bothered by such developments is keep your eye and mind on your goal – the glorious acropolis of Lindos.

Donkeys, with their drivers, can be hired (near the parking lot square), and those who must avoid exertion – especially if it is on a hot summer's day – should probably consider this means. But most people will find they approach the acropolis by stages. You wander through the village (following the arrows and the crowds) and come to the long, but for the most part, gradual stairway and path up to the outer gate. When you pass through this, you emerge onto a terraced area; there on the left, carved out of the rockface, is an exedra, or bench, crowned by a large relief of the stern of a ship, its lateral rudder and helmsman's seat clearly visible; the deck served as the pedestal for a statue of a priest of Poseidon (Hagesandros, son of Mikion, according to the inscription).

You ascend the long narrow stairway up to the main gate (where you must pay the admission fee), and then you enter into the remains of the **Government House of the Knights.** (The ruined chapel was a Byzantine **Church of St. John.)** Most people will push on quickly to the plateau to the south, with the remains of the **Sanctuary of Athena Lindia.**

You first see the portico, or stoa, with its double wings (actually added only about 200 BC); you then proceed up a monumental stairway and through what remains of the propylaea onto the higher level. Then at the far south corner stands what remains of the **temple to Athena** --four columns and part of the cella wall; these date from the second half of the 4th century BC but this temple is thought to be a fairly exact copy of an earlier temple on this very site.

But the acropolis of Lindos is not a place to worry about dates or architectural details: it is a locale to empathize with the ancient Greeks' sensation of being suspended between the sea and the sky, between earth and the gods. You can look down to the little pond-like harbor where St. Paul is said to have landed. Off to the northeast, is the promontory of Ayios Aemelianos, with the so-called Tomb of Kleoboulos: he was the tyrant who ruled Lindos in the 6th century BC who was also regarded as one of the Seven Sages of antiquity, and the tomb structure actually dates from centuries earlier. Meanwhile, on the slopes of a hill at the southern edge of the village can be seen the remains of an ancient theater.

Out of such incongruities arises the total experience of a visit to Lindos. Most visitors will be content to enjoy just the views and then head back –

with maybe some time set aside for a swim on the fine beach – to the city of Rhodes.

OTHER SITES ON RHODES

There are countless other places on Rhodes that reward the visitor who will spend the time to seek them out. There are public buses to many of these, but there is no denying that combining stops with the bus schedules can be quite time-consuming; in that respect, tour agency excursions or rented vehicles may be the preferred solution to seeing a lot in a limited time. In any case, here are some of the other attractions of Rhodes.

IALYSOS
PETALOUDES
("Valley of the Butterflies")
KAMEIROS

This trip encompasses three of the better-known destinations on Rhodes on what is essentially an excursion along the northwest coast of the island.

The drive south from the city of Rhodes along the first few miles of coast is past a series of hotels and beach resorts. At about 5 1/2 miles, you come to the village of **Trianda** (also known as Phile-rimos); a road off to the left climbs Mt. Philerimos for about 4 miles to its flat summit, the site of the acropo- 103 lis of **Ialysos,** one of the three major Dorian Greek cities of Rhodes. Even before these Dorian Greeks, however, it appears that Mycenaean Greeks had been here – for the acropolis was known in antiquity as **Achaia** and a Mycenaean cemetery was found on nearby slopes. And before the Mycenaeans, Phoenicians seem to have been established here. But it was between about 900 to 400 BC that Ialysos enjoyed its best years. Not all that much remains from this era except for a few elements of the temple to Athena Ialysia, from the 3rd-2nd centuries BC; and most imposing, a 4th century BC fountain in the Doric style, with the lions' heads from which the water flowed – hardly a major work but certainly an interesting one from this period.

Inevitably, the Knights of St John found this site, and they built a monastery and a church here, dedicated to St. Mary, or Our Lady of Philerimos; in the 20th century, the Italians virtually rebuilt these, so the structures are slightly artificial looking now. A path from the monastery leads to a ruined castle of the Knights. Suleiman II directed the final siege of Rhodes city from Ialysos.

Back on the main coast road south from Trianda, you pass through **Kremasti** (the site of an unusual festival, 14-23 August each year, one that includes sports, music, and dancing); south of here, by the way, is the airport of Rhodes. At about 11 miles (from the center of Rhodes), a turn to the left leads through a forested area into a valley with a stream through its middle: attracted by the scent of the storax, a small tree that gives a gum used by Roman Catholics for incense (and with seeds used to make rosaries), hundreds of thousands of butterflies gather here – mostly in July and August, so time your visit if this interests you: this is the much publicized **Valley of the Butterflies** (or **Petaloudhes** in Greek).

Back on the main coast road, at about 21 miles, a left turn leads (in just a half mile) to **Kameiros,** one of the three Doric Greek cities that established the city of Rhodes. Kameiros had neither an acropolis nor fortifications, and it eventually fell into ruins and oblivion; it was not until 1929 that Italians began to seriously excavate here, and they turned up a most extensive series of both public and domestic structures. The site – which charges a modest admission and observes hours – stretches down a slope above the coast, Ayios Minas Cape, while the public buildings are on the level area on high ground. The most impressive single remain is the long Doric stoa, or portico, built at the end of the 3rd century BC over a 6th-5th

The Remains of Camiros

105

Road leading to the Monastery of Filerimos

century BC reservoir. Still higher up are some remains of the temple of Athena. In the temenos, or sacred court, are the remains of a 3rd century Doric temple; above this extends the main street of the town, where there are several houses, including one with a

Monastery of Filerimos

peristyle court. As ancient Greek ruins go, nothing spectacular, but an unexpected site on Rhodes.

Back on the coast road, if you are still game, you might continue south past the ruins of **Kretinae** (said to have been founded by a Cretan) and on through the harbor of **Skala Kameiros**; from here you can get (occasional) boats to the offshore islands of **Alimnia** (with a ruined Byzantine-Crusador castle) and Khalki (about which, more later). Continuing on, you come to **Kritinia,** sited like an amphitheater and enjoying a fine view; on a nearby peak (425 feet) is a most impressive castle built by the Knights (about 1480) known as **Kastellos.**

The road turns inland after

Kritinia and leads in another 6 miles to Embona; this village is regarded as the best base for climbing **Mt. Atavyros,** at 3,986 feet the highest mountain on Rhodes. The ascent takes a good two hours – and there are no water sources, so bring your own. Once on the peak, you enjoy a fantastic view of the entire island. There are also some remains here, including those of the temple of Zeus Atavyros, one of the oldest temples known on Rhodes.

From Embona, the road circles around the foothills of Mt. Atavyros and on through Siana, a lovely village high on the mountains. From here a dirt road leads to the village of **Monolithos,** which is built in a terraced manner that allows for dramatic views; just outside the village, via a narrow footpath, on a large steep rock (known as Monopetra), sits the **Castle of Monolithos;** of medieval origin, its church has been thoroughly renovated. But if you have come this far, you are not interested in authentic architecture – you're swept away by the view.

If you had your own vehicle, you could continue on southward through the village of **Apolakia** and down to **Katavia,** regarded as the southernmost village on Rhodes; its tavernas are noted for serving fresh fish taken from the sea offshore. From Katavia, a rather rough path leads for some 7 miles down to Prassonissi, the southernmost point of Rhodes: at times the sand bridge here is covered by the water so leaving Prassonissi cut off like an island.

Again, if you have made it this far, you are presumably able to continue back north along the east coast via **Katavia** and then over towards the east coast and **Gennadi,** a village noted for its church of St. George as well as for the ample wild game – hare, snipe, and partridge – in its environs. Continuing north along the coast road some 2 miles, you would see a turnoff to the left to **Asklipion,** a mountain village with a medieval castle and a church dedicated to the Dormition of the Madonna (with a wall plaque inscribed with the year AD 1068). Back on the main coast road, you continue north via Lardos and Pilon past the turnoff, right, down to Lindos, and from here it is smooth passage back to the city of Rhodes.

Although this whole "circle route" around the island of Rhodes is just about 200 miles, it is not a trip that you'd want to make in a day – considering that long stretches of road aren't that good and that there are so many extraordinary sites and sights enroute. So schedule your time accordingly. Unless you're an experienced walker, you'll need your own wheels – and perhaps some camping equipment – to explore the southernmost part of Rhodes.

PROFITIS ELIAS

This can be a pleasant one-day excursion from the city of Rhodes, or it can be a locale to spend some time in, as there is a selection of hotels during the summer months, when Rhodians and Greeks come here to escape the heat. It is only some 30 miles from the city, but its wooded slopes and tranquil atmosphere make it seem like a world away. You get there by heading down along the west coast and at about 18 miles, at Kalavarda, before Kameiros, you take a turn off to the left and begin to climb the lower slopes; after about 10 miles, there is a turn to the left where you start up a curving ascent to about 2300 feet above sea level. The road passes through the Wood of the Prophet with its pines and cedars and cypresses – said to be especially heavy growth because of the

Hot springs of Callithea

The Valley of Butterflies

local belief that the Prophet Elias will kill anyone who fells a tree. There are also many wild deer in this area (not descendants of ancient denizens, but from the restocking by the Italians earlier in this country). The last few hundred feet to the summit of Profitis Elias (2620 feet) must be climbed by a trail. If you were to spend any time at the hotels here, there are some delightful villages in the nearby hills - Eleoussa (with a Byzantine Church of St. Nicholas), Platania, Ayios Isidoros, Laerma (with its nearby convent, Moni

Monastery of Chambica on the Eastern Coast of Rhodes

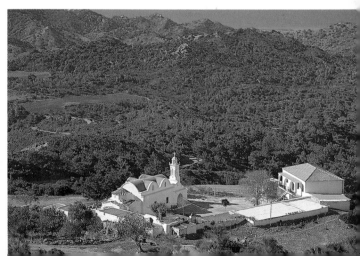

Thari), Profilia, and Mesanagros. It is part of Rhodes that few expect or see.

KALLITHEA

Another but still more accessible excursion from the city of Rhodes is to the baths of Kallithea, just some 6 1/2 miles southeast of the city, on the coast. The buildings from the Italian occupation are in a pseudo-Moorish style, with grottoes and gardens set amidst the rocks along the shore. "Taking the waters" here was once recommended for curing all kinds of ailments, but now people come simply to enjoy the beach.

KASTELLORIZO

Officially known as **Megisti** (from its ancient name, which means "largest" and refers to the fact that it is the largerst of its own little archipelago), Kastellorizo is actually an independent member of the Dodecannese (one of the 14 such), but those few foreigners who do visit it tend to include it as part of a sidetrip from Rhodes. It is linked by ship to the city of Rhodes - usually about two sailings a week, lasting some 8 hours - from which it is some 72 miles to the east; in fact, it is only about 1 1/2 miles off the Turkish coast, but despite its history of foreign occupations, it has somehow always remained a Greek island in its population ¹¹⁰ and orientation. Mycenaean

and Dorian Greeks settled here and the inhabitants worshipped Apollo; the Knights of St. John took it over in 1306, and it was under their Grand Master, Juan Fernando Heredia that the great castle was erected on the tiny island's rocky highpoint. (Because the rocks and soil have a slightly pinkish tinge, the island became known as Chastel-Roux, which became Kastellorizo - "red castle.") Over the centuries it fell under the King of Naples, the Turks, the Venetians, the Greeks (1823-33), the Turks again, then the Italians, and finally rejoined Greece in 1947.

The few hundred permanent inhabitants are concentrated in the capital, also known as Kastellorizo, or Megisti, on the east coast, where the ships put in. Because this was one of the few safe harbors along the coast of Asia Minor, Kastellorizo once prospered as a commercial port, but in this century most of its prosperity comes from emigrants. The island's soil doesn't support much agriculture, and the inhabitants depend on rainwater they must collect.

In the town of Kastellorizo, you will certainly want to visit the Cathedral of Saints Constantine and Helena, with its granite columns brought over from an ancient Temple of Apollo at Patara, in Lycia, Asia Minor. On the edge of town, too, is an impressive Lycian Tomb of the type found on the opposite coast of Asia Minor; cut into the natural rock, it has a Doric facade. And high over the town sits the Castle of the Knights (not to be confused with the Palaiokastro, the ancient fortress dating from the 3rd-2nd centuries BC).

Kastellorizo, only 3 1/2 square miles in area itself, boasts of 11 dependent islets, two of which — Rho and Strongyli — have lighthouse-keepers. (The widow who maintained the lighthouse on Rho by herself between 1938 and 1982, when she died at the age of 92, had raised the Greek flag each day at dawn and lowered each day at sunset for all those years; she was honored by the Greek government in 1975, but insisted on going back to Rho.)

Perhaps the main attraction of Kastellorizo for most who make it this far is its Blue Grotto; although not as well known as the Blue Grotto of Capri, it is in fact as large in area and even higher (its roof being some 65-80 feet). You would make the excursion from Kastellorizo, preferably in the late afternoon to take advantage of the reflected light within; it requires about three hours altogether.

There is also a fine swimming beach at Ayios Stephanos and on one of the dependent islets, Ayios Georgios (about a 10-minute ride by motorboat from Kastellorizo town).

"Treasure" of the Sea of Dodecannese

6 General Practical Information from A to Z

AIR TRAVEL

Within Greece, this is a monopoly of **Olympic Airways,** the national airline. **Olympic** has an excellent safety record. Almost all its flights originate in **Athens,** but there are some connecting routes (such as **Rhodes** and Crete in the tourist season). **Olympic** services all the major and more remote cities and islands of Greece with a variety of aircraft. During the tourist season, tremendous demands are placed on the service by the great numbers of foreigners, so you are advised to make reservations as far in advance as possible. You must be prepared for seasonal changes in schedules, too; and travel agents abroad will not always be up to date, so check your flights immediately upon arriving in Greece. Passengers who initiate their flights within Greece-may be limited to 15 kilos of luggage free of charge; those connecting with flights from abroad are allowed the international limits.

All Olympic flights, both international and domestic, operate out of the **West Air Terminal of Athens' Hellinikon Airport**; all other airlines use the **East Air Terminal.** The two are connected by frequent bus service, but about 45 minutes must be allowed to move from one to the other. Olympic also provides bus service from all its airports for a modest fee, but some people may find the wait not worth the money; especially if you are with a small group, a taxi can be relatively cheap. In **Athens** itself, the intown terminal for buses to and from the airport its too far from the center to walk there with luggage, but it is still considerably cheaper to take a taxi to this terminal and then the bus to the airport.

ALPHABET: See GREEK LANGUAGE

ANTIQUITIES: Greece enforces a very strict law against exporting antiques and antiquities. Anything dating from before 1830 is technically an antique and cannot be exported without official permission. This might be hard to prove in the case of a piece of textile or old jewelry, but the authorities are really interested in stopping the export of such items as ikons or manuscripts. As for genuine antiquities, small items are sold by several legitimate dealers, but permission for export must be obtained: the dealers should be able to direct you to the proper government office (which has traditionally been at the **National Archaeological Service, Leoforos Vassilissis Sofias 22, Athens**). Be wary of buying anything "under the counter": if it's not genuine, you're being cheated, and if it is genuine you're apt to find yourself in trouble.

AUTOMOBILE CLUB: Greece has a privately supported automobile club or association with offices in all main cities. Its Greek name forms the acronym **ELPA,** by which it is known; it means **Hellenic**

Touring and Automobile Club. Its head office is in **Athens** at the **Pyrgos Athinon** (corner of **Vassilissis Sofias** and **Mesogeion Ave**). It can assist you in obtaining an **International Driver's license** (so long as you have a valid license-which in practice is often accepted) or provide advice about insurance or other matters. For its members, **ELPA** provides a range of services, and its emergency repair vehicles will usually stop for any vehicle along the highway.

BABYSITTERS: Greeks have traditionally relied on their "extended families" to perform babysitting, but in recent years-due primarily to the needs of foreigners-Greek women have taken up this chore for money. They are not especially cheap, relative to wages in Greece and elsewhere, but they perform a necessary service. If you need a babysitter, contact the hotel reception desk, the **Tourist Police,** a travel agency, or the **National Tourist Information office.** The higher grade hotels should almost certainly be able to provide someone.

BANKS· There is no shortage of banks in Greek cities. Their normal hours are 8 AM to 2 PM, Monday through Friday, and some open for at least foreign exchange on Saturday mornings, Sunday morning and late afternoon or early evening. But banks do close on the main Greek holidays (See HOLIDAYS), so make sure you do not leave vital transactions to those days. Most goodsized banks maintain separate counters and windows for foreign exchange so be sure you get in the right line. Banks officially-and generally in practice do-give the best exchange rate (and usually give a slightly better rate for travelers' checks than for foreign currency). If you have bought too many Drachmas and want to buy back your own currency, you must provide the receipts of the Drachma purchases, and even so you will be limited as to how much you can convert back. You may be asked for your passport in any bank transactions, so have it with you. See also MONEY.

BARBERS: There are plenty of barbers in Greece, and you shouldn't need much language to get what you want. It is customary to tip the barber about 10%; if he uses a boy for cleaning up, you give him a few extra Drachma. See also HAIRDRESSERS.

BATHING: See SWIMMING

BICYCLES FOR RENT: Bicycles may be rented-usually from renters of motorbikes, motorscooters, etc.-in the main cities and resort centers. Rates vary, but they obviously become cheaper over longer periods. And if you are planning on renting for a specific trip on a specific occasion, reserve in advance, especially during the main tourist season. See also MOTORBIKES FOR RENT

BUS TRAVEL: There is frequent public bus service both within all large Greek cities and connecting main cities to smaller villages. In the cities, you pay as you get on the bus at the rear; keep your receipt for possible inspection. For intercity travel, you usually buy the ticket at the starting point; the ticket may include a numbered seat-but Greeks often pay little attention to this. However, especially during the main tourist season, buses can quickly become crowded, so you are advised to buy your ticket as soon as possible. Schedules between main cities and outlying villages have usually been set up for the convenience of villagers who need to come into the city early in the morning and return home late afternoon, so tourists may have to plan around such schedules. If you want to get a bus at a stop along its route, be sure that you signal clearly to the approaching driver, who may not otherwise stop.

CAMPING: Officially there is no longer camping in Greece except at the locales set aside either for government or commercial campsites. The **National Tourist Organization** has a brochure listing all such places around Greece. Such campsites, like those elsewhere, offer a range of support services, from hot water to electric outlets to food. Unofficially, there is still some camping-whether in vehicles or tents-on various beaches and fields. If you do try this, at least respect the property and dispose of all your wastes in approved ways. If you didn't stay too long in one place and picked fairly remote locales, you might get away with such camping.

CAR RENTAL: There are many firms that rent cars-both the wellknown international agencies such as **Hertz** and **Avis** and many locally owned firms-in all the large cities and resort centers around Greece. Rates are generally controlled by law, and variations are supposed to reflect different services, etc. The bigger international agencies, for example, can offer pickups and dropoffs at airports; they are also better equipped to provide quick replacement vehicles should something go wrong. Actual rates vary greatly depending on the size of vehicle, length of time, etc. You will find that it is much easier to rent a car if you have a charge card; otherwise you must leave a large deposit. You will probably want to pay the extra charge for full-coverage insurance (that is, to eliminate any problems with minor damage to the vehicle). You must produce a valid driver's license -in practice, this is accepted without the **International Driver's License.** Do volunteer the names of all individuals who may be driving the vehicle. And during the main tourist season, make your reservation as far in advance as possible.

CHARTER CRUISES: This has become a most popular way of visiting the **Greek islands.** Cruises vary from 2 days to a week or longer, and sometimes include stops at other **Mediterranean ports** (e.g. **Ephesus** or **Constantinople** in **Turkey**). They are not especially cheap, but considering that you save on hotel rooms and have to eat someplace, and that the alternatives (less comfortable small interisland ships or expensive airplanes) do not appeal to many people, these cruises become the best choice for many people. The principal disadvantage is the short time allowed on shore in most cases. Most of these cruises originate in **Athens-Piraeus,** but inquire at any travel agent for information.

CHURCHES: Since about 98% of all Greeks belong to the Greek Orthodox Church, it is not surprising that most churches will be of that faith. Visitors to Greece should make a point of stepping into some of these churches, whether old or new, large or small; best time is when a service is being held-even better when some special holy day or occasion such as a wedding or baptism is being celebrated. (Greeks are happy to see foreigners in attendance.) It used to be possible to step into any remote chapel, but with an increase of thefts of ikons and valuables in recent years, many chapels are now kept locked; usually the key is held by the priest or someone else in the nearest village. There are small pockets of **Roman Catholics in Greece** - in the **Ionian, Dodecannese,** and **Cycladic islands,** and of course a large foreign community in Athens - and services are held in their own churches. There are relatively few **Protestants in Greece,** and most of these are foreigners in **Athens,** where there are several **Protestant churches.** There are also Jewish synagogues in **Athens** and **Thessaloniki.**

CIGARETTES and CIGARS: Greeks continue to smoke cigarettes as though cancer had never been invented. The Greek cigarettes (and they grow a great deal of tobacco) come in all strengths and prices, and determined smokers should be able to find a brand to substitute for their otherwise very expensive favorites from home. There are limits on how many can be imported free of duty into Greece: 200 cigarettes, 50 cigars (or 200 grams of tobacco for a pipe).

CLOTHING: If you come during the hot months-May through September-you can get by in most situations with a light wardrobe. Do bring at least a sweater for cool evenings, however. And of course if you intend to spend time at higher elevations, you must bring adequate clothing-for cooler weather, possible rain, and any special requirements (such as rugged shoes for hiking). Greeks are informal dressers, and at beaches almost anything goes; however, they do not like to see people wearing beachwear in towns or in stores away from the beach; villagers are especially conservative, and you will create unnecessary comments if you parade around villages in scanty beachwear. You can always buy needed clothing in Greece, but it is not especially cheap. There are some local specialties, of course-informal shirts, shawls or sweaters, sandals, sunhats, etc.

COMPLAINTS: With literally millions of foreigners moving around Greece each year, it is impossible not to have occasional incidents or cases of dissatisfaction. Many of these arise from language problems or cultural differences. But if you feel you have a legitimate complaint, there are several possibilities. Start with the local **Tourist Police** or **National Tourist Organization office:** the emergency **phone number** for the **Tourist Police** all over Greece is **171.** Athens has a special number for handling complaints by foreigners: **135.** One way to stop possible episodes is to ask for an itemized bill or receipt that you can indicate you intend to show to the **Tourist Police.**

CONSULATES and EMBASSIES: All the major nations of the world maintain embassies in Athens, but most travelers are more apt to need help in some more remote city. Many countries maintain consulates in other Greek cities-and often in unexpected cities, due to levels of commerce or tourism in these areas. Many of these consuls are local nationals, but they are authorized to help. Likewise, even if your own country does not maintain a consulate in a particular city, another country's might be able to help if it primarily a matter-at least at the outset-of finding someone who speaks your language. (Example: You need someone to translate a Greek document.)

CREDIT CARDS: The major international and certain national credit cards are accepted in many situations around Greece. The expected scale of acceptance prevails: the more expensive and more internationally-oriented the facility (hotel, restaurant, store), the more likely they are to honor credit cards. You cannot expect small tavernas, little pensions, village shops, to honor such cards. In most cases, those places that honor credit cards display plaques or signs so indicating at the front. And in the case of car rentals, credit cards are actually preferred for they serve to assure the agencies of your credit standing. See also TRAVELERS CHECKS

CUSTOMS CONTROL: For the mass of foreigners who visit Greece, customs control is so relaxed that it will hardly be noticed. You will have to pass through passport and customs control on your first point of entry into Greece-for most people, this will mean **Athens, Piraeus,** or one of the border checkpoints at the north, or **Patras.** There are some limits, however, and although you might slip in uninspected, you should know of these. You can bring in unlimited sums of travellers checks or foreign currency, but you are limited to bringing in (and taking out) 1,500 Drachmas. Only 200 cigarettes or 50 cigars or 200 grams of tobacco can be brought in; 1 liter of liquor or 1 liter of wine may be imported. Cameras, typewriters, radios, tape-recorders may be brought in as long as they are clearly for personal use; there are some limits on weapons and you should inquire before setting out for Greece. You cannot import explosives or narcotics (or parrots!). In leaving, you are limited to how much olive oil you can take out tax-free (as well as to 1,500 Drachmas and antiques before 1830-and antiquities without official permission: See ANTIQUITIES).

DENTISTS: Dentists are to be found in all large to middle-sized cities. Most have trained abroad (and so will speak at least one foreign language) and they will usually have quite modern equipment. Their rates should be quite reasonable. When in need of a dentist, start by asking at the hotel reception desk (especially at the better grade hotels) or the **Tourist Police:** for one thing, someone can then phone ahead and explain your problem.

DOCTORS: Doctors are found in all large to middle-sized cities, although various specialists may be found only in the former. Most of these doctors will have done some of their studies abroad and so will speak at least one foreign language. Their knowledge, equipment, and techniques will be thoroughly up to date. In **Athens** especially, you must expect to pay international rates; elsewhere doctors may be somewhat cheaper. Incidentally, if you had a medical emergency in a small or remote locale, the local people would certainly help in getting a doctor to you or you to a doctor. See also PHARMACIES.

DRIVING IN GREECE: Large numbers of foreigners now drive either their own or rented vehicles around Greece. In both cases you need a **valid driver's licence,** and theoretically you should have an **International Driver's License.** It if it is your own car you are bringing into Greece, you need its registration (or log book) and you need proof of adequate insurance. There will be limits (usually about 4 months) on the length of time you can drive your car in Greece; you can usually get an extension (for 8 months) to continue driving your car without any major registration fees. The car will be entered in your passport, so if you were for any reason want to sell it in Greece, you must make very sure you are in full compliance with Greek laws governing such transactions.

Your car-and all rented vehicles - are exempt from the Greek law governing alternate Sunday regulations (even number plates-odd number plates). But foreigners must obey speed limits (and police can demand payment of fines on the spot) and you should observe parking regulations: the Greek custom is for police to remove license plates-and then force you to go around to a police station to pay the fine to get your plates back!

Fuel of all grades is available all over Greece-at some of the highest rates in the world. Because almost all Greeks drive imported cars (some foreign vehicles are now being assembled in Greece), there is no problem obtaining spare parts or experienced repairmen for your vehicle. (You may be amazed at the age of some of the boys who work on your vehicle-under adult supervision, you hope.)

Driving is on the right. Roads are not always well marked for danger spots or unusual conditions: curves, soft shoulders, fallen rocks, steep gradients-these are often not indicated. And although Greece has built up an impressive national highway system, many roads are in need of basic maintenance: it is not uncommon to encounter major potholes or rough stretches in the middle of otherwise decent highways. In addition, Greek drivers themselves retain a few habits from the days before motor vehicles were so common: they turn into main highways, stop along the road without warning, weave in and out in city streets. (Greece has one of the highest fatality rates from driving accidents.) But with basic caution, you should have no trouble driving in Greece.

DRUGS: Greek authorities take a very strict approach on importing drugs. On the other hand, Greek men in certain locales do smoke marijuana and use even stronger drugs. But foreigners would be advised to have nothing to do with drugs while in Greece.

DRYCLEANING: There are plenty of drycleaning establishments in all large to medium-sized cities. It is relatively cheap and fast-you should be able to get your clothing back within the day if you bring it early and make your needs clear. See also LAUNDRY.

EARTHQUAKES: Despite the publicity that attends earthquakes in Greece-from the days of **Lost Atlantis** to the ones that struck the **Athens area** in 1980 – these need not be of concern to visitors. The odds are that the most anyone will experience might be a slight tremor. One might just as well stay away from **Italy**-or **California,** for that matter.

EASTER: In many respects, **Easter** is the major occasion of the Greek year. Many Foreigners deliberately time their visit to Greece so as to be able to experience some of the events associated with the **Greek Easter.** Because it does not usually coincide with the **Easter** celebrated in the **Western Christian churches,** care must be taken that you do not arrive at the wrong time. The **Greek Orthodox Easter** is calculated as follows: it must fall after the first full moon following the first day of spring (as is true with Western Christian Easter) but it must also fall after the **Jewish Passover.** This then affects the

Lent period-including the two weeks before **Lent** known as Carnival, with its festivities and parades, culminating in **Clean Monday,** with its vegetarian feast and kite-flying. And of course **Good Friday** depends on Easter's date: this is marked by a funeral procession through the streets. Saturday evening involves a church service that ends at midnight with the lighting of candles. **Easter Sunday** itself is an occasion for feasting and festivities. And even the Monday after is observed as a holiday. Ideally you should try to get invited to some village where the traditional **Easter** is observed, but even in the large cities there is enough to make a stranger feel the full impact of Easter on Greeks.

ELECTRICITY: Greece has now converted to A(lternating) C(urrent) at 220 voltage. This means that **Americans** must have converters for their 110-115 volt electrical appliances. Furthermore Greek outlets and plugs vary considerably from both **American** and many **European** standard types, so converters may be required. But electricity is virtually everywhere in Greece.

EMBASSIES: See CONSULATES AND EMBASSIES

EMERGENCIES: For emergency help of any kind, you will get a response 24 hours a day (and hopefully in a language you can speak) by dialing either the **Tourist Police (171)** or the regular police, **(100)** anywhere in Greece. (However, in smaller towns and villages, you will first have to dial the code to the nearest large city). Another possibility is to get to a hotel's reception desk and ask them to make the first call.

FISHING: There is relatively little freshwater fishing in most parts of Greece-and the saltwater fishing in the Mediterranean is not as good as one might assume. But Greeks do catch fish, obviously. No license is required. Nor is any license required for underwater speargun fishing: however, you must be at least 200 meters (667 feet) away from any other people in the water.

FOOD AND DRINK: Whatever else people come to Greece to enjoy, they all spend fair amount of their time in ating and drinking. And since ood and drink end up being mong the main ingredients-and usually pleasures-of a Greek holiday, certain things might be said to improve their chances of being enjoyed.

To start with the first meal, breakfast-in most hotels this will be the "continental" type: coffee, possibly some sort of juice, bread, butter, and jelly. Unfortunately, all too often these are less than exciting. If you are required to take breakfast as part of your hotel's rates, that's that. But if you have a choice, you might consider going out and assembling your own breakfast: buying fresh fruit, buying your own roll or cheese pie or sweet, and then taking nothing but coffee in a cafe. Depending on your personal preference, you can take your large dinner at noon or in the evening, as most Greek restaurants offer the same menu, noon and night. (Only the more luxurious restaurants prepare a more elaborate menu for the even-

ing.) But consider: if you intend to move about in the heat of the afternoon, you should probably eat light. Then treat yourself to something refreshing late afternoon. For Greeks eat their evening meal late-anything before 8 PM is considered early. Another variation is to assemble your own picnic for the noon meal-fresh fruits, bread, cheeses, sliced meats or sardines, etc. And when ordering meals in restaurants, you are welcome to go back to the kitchen area to inspect and point out exactly what you want (and don't hesitate to send back anything that is not what you want). If you do not care for much olive oil, indicate that you want little or no **ladhi.** And if you find the food tepid to cold, indicate that you want your food served **zestós.** (If you're lucky, they'll get it as hot as you prefer it).

Greeks like to eat snacks when drinking anything alcoholic. Shrimp, tomato slices, bits of cheese, artichoke leaves - these are known as **mezés** or **mezedákis**; similar hors d'oeuvres as part of a full meal are **orektiká. Mezés** can be had at almost any little cafe or snack place. Sweets and ice cream **(pagotá)** are obtained at special sweethshops and cafés. Traditionally, Greeks go to these places for desserts, which are not available at typical restaurants.

Coffee was not traditionally served at restaurants, either, but now, to satisfy their many foreign patrons, some restaurants have taken to serving coffee. You must specify whether you want **ellenikós kafés** or **"American"** (or **"French"**) coffee; the latter will usually be 119 powdered coffee, while the former is what is widely known abroad as the Turkish style-a small cup with the muddy coffee taking up about the bottom third of the cup. The sugar is boiled with the coffee and you must specify the degree of sweetness you want: medium is **métrios**, sweet in **glykó**, light is **me olighi**, and no sugar at all is **skétos**. Tea is aviable, too. And Greeks usually take a glass of cold water with everything they eat or dring. Beer is a popular drink-there are several brands brewed in Greece that are quite decent. As for wines, the native Greek wines certainly can't compete with the world's better varieties, but some are adequate. There is first of all a choice between the **retsina**-wines that have been stored in "resinated" barrels and thus have a mild turpentine(!) flavor: not to everyone's taste, but in fact they go well with the Greek menu-and the **aretsinoto** wines. In addition to the usual whites, pinks, and reds, there are sweet dessert wines and quite good Greek brandies. There is also the Greek **oúzo,** made from distilling the crushed mash after the juice has been pressed from the grapes and then adding a slight anisette flavor.

Above all, whether eating or drinking, in fancy restaurants or simple tavernas, everyone should occasionally experiment with some of the different items on the Greek menu. Don't stay in the rut with the same **moussaká** and Greek salad

See also RESTAURANTS. And for a discussion of special foods and drinks of Rhodes, see page 42.

GREEK LANGUAGE: The Greek language is far too complex and subtle to even begin to be taught or learned in a book like this. But there are a few basics that can be conveyed. Elsewhere (pages 188) a short list of words and phrases are provided to help the traveler in the more common situations.

The Written language: Most visitors to Greece will have little to do with written Greek except to attempt to read signs, menus, etc. Greek pronunciation is difficult enough so that its finer points could involve long discussions. Here is the alphabet with the English equivalent of the most common sounds so that at least a start can be made on reading Greek.

The Spoken language: Acquiring even the most basic spoken Greek is difficult or not, depending on an individual's skill in picking up a foreign language. But because of the unfamiliar alphabet, many foreigners get easily discouraged: there is not that gratuitous gain that comes from just looking at words in some foreign languages and gradually realizing that you can figure out meanings. Yet anyone should be able to rely on their ear and then try to approximate pronunciations. Greeks are genuinely appreciative of any such efforts. One problem, however, that Greeks have ignoring: their language depends so much on the accent's falling on the precise syllable that this becomes at least as important as the purity of the sound. When in doubt, try shifting the accent until you hit the proper syllable.

The casual traveler need not become concerned about the

historical rivalries between the "pure" and demotic spoken Greek: the demotic will be fine for all situations. Likewise, although there are numerous dialects spoken in various parts of Greece-some quite different in pronunciation and vocabulary-the foreigner will be doing fine just to speak a basic Greek. Put another way, dialect variations are the least of a foreigner's problems!

GUIDES AND INTER-PRETERS: Officially licensed guides can be provided from the **National Tourist Organization offices** or by the bigger travel agents. Their fees are also officially controlled-and depend on such factors as the time involved, the number in the party, the difficulty of the excursion, etc. Tours organized by travel agencies, of course, usually provide guides who speak the language(s) of the majority of the foreigners taking the tour. If you are lucky, you will get a guide who

HAIRDRESSERS: There are many hairdressers in all large to medium-sized Greek cities. You can get a complete line of services. Tipping is expected-perhaps 10% for the principal hairdresser, half that for the assistant.

HITCHHIKING: As long as basic precautions are observed, hitchhiking (also known to Europeans as "autostop") is generally allowed throughout Greece. Young women, whether alone or in pairs, should exercise special judgment as to the rides they accept.

HOLIDAYS: There are two types of holidays that tourists will want to know about while in Greece. One includes the national holidays when not only all banks, museums, archaeological sites, almost all stores, and even many restaurants are closed. These are the following days:

January 1-	New Year's day
January 6-	Epifhany
Last Monday before Lent	
Good Friday	Movable dates (**See EASTER**)
Easter Sunday	
Easter Monday	
March 25	Greek Independence Day
May 1	Spring Festival, or May Day
August 15-	Assumption of the Virgin Mary
October 28-	Okhi (No!) Day
	(Second World War incident)
December 25-	Christmas Day

not only is comfortable with your language but has a true command of the subject-that is, you will get much more than a mechanical-rote recitation of facts.

But it addition to these national holidays, there are numerous local holidays and festivals-in honor of some historical or patriotic event, a saint, an age-old festival. In 121 particular, "name-days" are major occasions when the saint's name is one of the more popular ones: people with that name often come from great distances to a monastery, chapel, or village where that saint is especially honored. Sometimes Greek festivities go on for two or more days, involving dancing and feasting. Foreigners are traditionally welcomed, and anyone with a taste for such occasions should inquire from the **National Tourist Organization office** or **Tourist Police** - or, for that matter, from almost any Greek who seems informed-about any forthcoming holiday of this kind. See also HOURS, EASTER.

HOSPITALITY: Greek hospitality is legendary, and it usually lives up to its reputation, especially in more remote villages and where only a few foreigners are involved. But in recent years, with the influx of literally millions of foreigners annually, there has inevitably been some pulling back: there is no way that Greeks can "relate to" every single foreigner who crosses paths with them, let alone afford to extend the full panoply of traditional hospitality. However, arrive in a small party in a remote village and you may still be treated as a special guest-offered special drinks and food, presented with little gifts when you leave. Greek males still usually insist on paying for meals when they take a foreigner to a favorite eating place. You will often be offered a coffee or cold drink when visiting with a Greek-and the Greeks present will expect you to accept even as they refuse anything for them-

selves. But this hospitality works both ways. Greeks in these situations will often question foreigners about fairly personal matters-why a married couple doesn't have children, how much money you have paid for certain items. And once the preliminaries are underway, Greeks expect you to participate to the end: if they have begun to plan a meal for you, they would be genuinely hurt if you ran off to save them the trouble and expense. So don't embark on these encounters unless you are prepared to enjoy them all the way.

HOSPITALS: All large, medium-sized, and even some quite small towns have hospitals or at least clinics. You might go direct to one if you have some medical emergency. Only in the larger cities, of course, could you expect to find a full range of services and specialists. Greek hospitals provide minimal nursing care: a member of the family will often bed down next to the patient to provide full attention, meals, etc. Most foreigners will never have any contact with hospitals, but if you had to you will find that they are quite adequate. See also DOCTORS, EMERGENCIES.

HOSTELS: There are **Youth Hostels** throughout Greece - in most major cities and also in tourist centers. You will almost certainly be asked to produce a membership card from a recognized Youth Hostel association; if you do not have one from your home country, you can join (for a fee) the **Greek Youth Hostels Association** (at 4 Dragatsaniou

Street, Athens). There is usually a limit of 5 days on your stay at these hostels.

HOTELS: There are hotels to suit all tastes and all pocketbooks all over Greece. If you have particular preferences as to price, location, or other specifics, you should reserve in advance for the main tourist season: no one ever spends the night on the street, but you cannot be certain of getting the exact hotel you want. At other times of the year, however, there is generally a surplus of beds. All hotel and room accommodations in Greece are quite strictly controlled-as to price, conditions, etc.-by the government. There are various classes, or categories, of hotels, form Deluxe and then Class A through E; the criteria may not always seem important to all guests (e.g. size of public rooms, telephones in rooms), but in general the categories reflect the levels of amenities. Many tourists find the Class C hotels-most of which are relatively new-quite adequate (and they cost about one-half a Class A hotel and two-thirds a Class B). The prices are supposed to be posted in each room, but sometimes it is hard for a hotel to keep up with all seasonal changes.

Ask for the price of the room before you agree to anything (and then ask to inspect it , if you care to). Find out if the price quoted includes all taxes and whether it includes any meals: hotels are allowed to require clients to take breakfast, if offered by the hotel, and the Class B, A, and Deluxe hotels may also require clients to take at least one other meal if the hotel maintains a dining room. Service charges should be included in the price quoted, but you may want to tip a bit extra anyone who has done you any personal favors. Prices may be raised during the "high" tourist season (and may be lowered during the off season); hotels can also charge an extra 10% if you stay less than three nights. It all sounds quite complicated, but in practice you are told a price of a room and that's usually the end of it. Do clarify the various possibilities, however, if you are concerned.

HOURS: Greek shop hours can be a quite complicated subject, but in general stores open at 8 AM and close around 1:30 or 2 PM, Monday through Saturday; on several days a week (but not Saturday) some shops reopen again from about 5 to 8:30 PM. Inquire in the morning if you have any special needs for that day. And of course all shops observe the national holidays. See HOLIDAYS.

HUNTING: Foreigners may hunt within Greece but only with a license and with limitations on seasons, type of game, etc. There are also limits on the types of weapons and ammunition you can bring in. Inquire at the **National Tourist Organization** or a **Greek Embassy** abroad if this is to be an important part of your visit to Greece.

INFORMATION: There are various sources for detailed information about Greece. Abroad, there are the **Greek Embassies** and **Consulates;** the **National Tourist Organization** maintains offices in many of 123 the principal cities of the world; and travel agents have some types of touristic information. Within Greece, there are the various offices of the **National Tourist Organization,** the **Tourist Police,** and also the travel agencies. One of the problems for all of these offices is to keep up with the many changes from year to year and from season to season in schedules, prices, etc. Thus, not until you actually get to Greece can you probably find out exact times and costs of the sailings to the many Greek islands; what you should be able to learn while still abroad is whether such service is usually available.

LAUNDRY: Laundry can usually be placed at a drycleaning establishment to be picked up within 24 hours, and the better class hotels usually will take care of laundry for their clients. But wherever it is done, it will seem expensive (especially relative to so many other costs in Greece). But every item will be neatly ironed, and in some situations this service may be a necessary expense. There are almost no self-service laundries anywhere in Greece-there has been one in the **Plaka** section of **Athens.** Most tourists simply make do by washing out things in their rooms and then hanging them on the usually present balcony.

LUGGAGE: Greek air terminals and bus stations usually do not provide any place to leave luggage for even short periods of time. Tourists are left to make their own arrangements-with a cafe, restaurant, hotel, store, or wherever. Offer a reasonable sum for the service, and although it cannot be legally guaranteed, your luggage should always be safe.

MEDICINES: See PHARMACIES

MENU: See RESTAURANTS

MONEY: The basic Greek currency is the Drachma. The Lepta-100 make up a Drachmahas all but vanished from common usage, although occasionally prices are quoted with a 50 Lepta. (When Greek shopkeepers or others lack small change, they automatically "round off"-sometimes to your advantage, sometimes to theirs). The exchange rate of the Drachma with various foreign currencies has been fluctuating so in recent years that it would be misleading to provide specific figures here. As soon as you find out the exchange rate for your own national currency, calculate some basic equivalencies-that is, what does 5 Drachmas, equal, 10 Drachmas, 50 Drachmas, etc. This will provide a general sense of what things are costing. Technically you are limited to importing (and exporting) 1,500 Drachmas in currency; most foreigners are never even questioned, let alone inspected, but there is no real "black market" in Greek currency and little opportunity for most people to gain anything by violating the law. See also BANKS.

MOTORBIKES FOR RENT: Motorbikes may be rented from various agents in the main cities and resort centers. Rates vary but they obviously become cheaper over longer periods. During the main tourist season and over holidays, you should probably reserve in advance. To rent a motorbike, however, you must be at least 18 years of age and licensed to operate one. You (and any passengers) must wear a protective helmet. And you should carry all the insurance you can get. See also BICYCLES FOR RENT.

MOUNTAINEERING: It may be overlooked-considering that most people come to Greece to enjoy the beaches and water-that Greece also has many fine mountains that offer challenging and enjoyable possibilities. There is a **Greek Mountainclimbing Club** (EOS is the Greek acronym), with branches in many cities, and foreigners are made to feel welcome on their excursions and in their facilities. They maintain various huts on major mountains. Although the peaks may not seem that high by world standards, the weather conditions often make some of the ascents quite difficult, and certainly no one should set out to climb unless properly equipped and experienced. Consult the **National Tourist Organization** for details about contacting a local mountaineering club or obtaining a local guide.

MOVIES: No one would ever travel to Greece to see a movie-the selection, even in **Athens,** is usually dismal, and in smaller cities it is hard to know where such movies have come from. But there are times when someone might want to retreat to a movie, and during the summer, when there are many outdoor movie theaters, it can be quite pleasant to sit under the starry Mediterranean sky and sit back and enjoy a movie you'd feel guilty about

seeing at home. Most foreign films in Greece are shown in their original language and with Greek subtitles, but ask to make sure before you enter.

NEWSPAPERS AND MAGAZINES: There is a large selection of foreign-language (that is, non-Greek) newspapers and magazines to be found in the large and medium-sized cities and also in all tourist centers. Athens has an English-language daily, **The Athens News,** and a fine English-language monthly, **The Athenian.** There is also a good selection of papers and periodicals brought in from abroad; they tend to be expensive (compared to prices at home) and the news will seem a bit dated (when you first arrive), but the longer you stay the more you may appreciate these links with the world.

PARKING: There was once a time when there were so few cars that finding a parking place was no problem in Greece. Then came a phase when the car population "exploded" so fast they took over every available sidewalk and corner. Now the Greek police have begun to fight back: in Athens and some cities, the police remove the license plates when your car is in violation and you must go to the local stationhouse and pay the fine to retrieve your plates. Meters are appearing in some cities. Parking restrictions are generally enforced, for foreigners as well as Greeks. Athens and several other cities and tourist centers have set aside a few places for tourist parking (marked by signs) but during the main season these are as 125 hard to find free as any other places.

PASSPORTS AND VISAS: A valid national passport is all that is required of most visitors to Greece-although you will probably be asked to fill out an entry card on the airplane or ship-so long as you are a transient: This period varies (depending on recipro-cal arrangements with the individual's home country), but for **British** and **Common-wealth** subjects this is three months and for **Americans,** two months. For longer stays, visas must be applied for: Inquire at the **Tourist Police** or **National Tourist Organization** as to how to proceed.

PENSIONS: These are a cheaper, more basic type of accommodation to be found in locales where a lot of travelers pass through. You probably won't have a private toilet or bath, and the buildings will usually be older, but linen will be clean and some people prefer the more homey atmos-phere. Breakfast is usually available at a pension. See also ROOMS TO RENT.

PHARMACIES: Pharmaci-es, drugstores, or chemists, there are plenty of them around Greece and they carry a fairly full selection of pres-cription drugs as well as general health, sanitary, and cosmetic items. (A pharmacy is usually clearly marked by a **red Maltese cross.**) There will always be at least one pharma-cy open, 24 hours a day, in any large city: the closed ones should have a sign in their window indicating which one is open. If you have special medical needs, of course, you had better make arrangements

with your own doctor at home before setting off.

PHOTOGRAPHY: Greece is famed as a photographer's paradise, what with its light and subjects. There are plenty of shops selling films and camera supplies-but all are expensive and you are advised to bring your own. You can get your films developed in relati-vely short times. In traveling about Greece, be careful to observe the occasional restric-tions against photographing in areas of military bases.

POLICE: See EMERGEN-CIES

POST OFFICE: Any good-sized city will have its post office, and larger cities will have several branch offices. They keep varied hours, but best is to get there in the morning. Some will open for only limited service in the late afternoon-postage stamps or for **Poste Restante.** (This latter refers to mail addressed to someone with no other known or fixed address-what Ameri-cans know as **General Delive-ry.**) Postage rates vary consi-derably (and rise inevitably) depending on the nature of the item (post card, letter, etc.), the weight, the destination, etc. The best is to know the basic stamps for most of your mail (that is, air mail post cards to your homeland, the lightest air mail letters, etc.) and be prepared to have any mail in question weighed. Stamps can often be purchased at certain stationery shops but you will pay a slight surcharge for the privilege.

PRICES: The one thing certain is that they will rise over time, in Greece as elsewhere. Some prices, however, do come down during the off-season-hotels in particular. By and large, prices are well marked for most items you will be purchasing, whether food in the market, or clothes in a store, and Greeks do not appreciate your trying to negotiate prices. If a shopkeeper sees you about to leave he may make some kind of a reduction or offer, but he does not want you to turn every purchase into a bazaar haggling.

RADIO: There are several possibilities for foreigners who like to keep up with the news via radio and in their own language. Greek stations provide at least one brief program daily with news and weather in **English, French,** and **German.** The American Armed Forces Radio broadcasts 24 hours daily, with frequent news updates. And there is the **BBC** overseas and the **Voice of America.**

REDUCTIONS: There are some reductions in admissions to museums and archaeological sites but they are limited to special groups. Foreign students of subjects directly related to the world of Greek art and archaeology can get a pass that allows for a 50% reduction to all national sites and museums (not to locally run). Students who present an **International Student Identity Card** are granted a reduced fee at some places. And a very special group of archaeologists, professors of art and architecture and classical subjects, museum professionals, **UNESCO** and some other government officials are given free entry to sites and muse-

ums. If you think you qualify, go to the **Directorate of Antiquities,** 14 Aristidou St., Athens, with proper identification and find out how to comply.

RELIGION: See CHURCHES

RESTAURANTS: There is no problem in finding a restaurant in Greece, and although they range from the quite elaborate and expensive to the rather dingy and cheap, most foreigners end up patronizing a relatively narrow spectrum. They are officially classed, and this affects the prices they are allowed to charge. The easy way to approach a restaurant is to make sure its appearance appeals and then look at some standard item on the menu-which should always be posted out front-and see how its price compares with the same item in other places you've eaten in. Not necessarily, but usually, if the moussaka or Greek salad is expensive, then everything will be expensive. Once you have decided to eat there, go to the kitchen area and select your foods-most proprietors are happy to have you do so; this eliminates the need for a lot of talking and the possibility of some unwanted surprises. Send back food if it is not what you want. The standard printed Greek menu has its prices listed in two columns: that on the left is the price before the obligatory service charge, that on the right includes the service percentage-and it is the latter you will be billed for. It is customary, even so, to tell the waiter to keep a small extra sum when he presents the change; and if there was a "waterboy" for your table you leave a few Drachmas for him.

ROOMS TO RENT: In some of the more crowded tourist centers individual families have taken to renting rooms in their homes. They are supposed to be supervised so that basic sanitary practices are observed, no matter how simple the accommodation. They are relatively cheap and many people find such rooms adequate. See also PENSIONS

SAILING: See YACHTS

SHOESHINE: In the larger cities, young boys or even men will be shining shoes in various public areas. Agree on the price beforehand-and if you are in doubt, ask a Greek to help establish the cost. A small tip is customary.

SHOPPING AND SOUVENIRS: In the largest and even in relatively small cities of Greece, you will be able to purchase almost any item you need for your stay in Greece. Often as not it will even be your favorite brand, since Greeks import virtually everything: your favorite suntan lotion, your preferred instant coffee-they'll probably be available. But these are not what most people come to Greece to buy. It is the souvenirs and specialties of Greece that interest most travelers, and here the selection is almost overwhelming, especially in the major tourist centers. Since everyone's taste differs as to what constitutes a suitable souvenir, there is no use laying down rules. Take your time and look around: it is not that shops cheat but simply that prices often will be 128 lower in one place than another-and sometimes the lowest price will be in some unexpected location. (Even then, the difference may be relatively few Drachmas, so you must ask yourself how much of your limited time you want to spend in comparison shopping.) It is difficult to find genuine handmade artifacts, but they are available, and often not that much more expensive than the massproduced items. Often it is the smaller and less centrally located shops that have the unusual items, so leave the main streets lined with gift shops and go looking. Even then, don't give too much credence to claims of age or uniqueness or "the last one left...": just buy what you like at the price you feel you want to pay. See also PRICES and HOURS.

SPORTS: Those who like to include active sports in their vacations and travels will find many opportunities to do so in Greece. In the winter, for instance, there are several ski lifts operating (most of them in central and northern Greece, but one in the White Mountains of Crete). There are several golf clubs in Greece (near **Athens,** and on **Rhodes** and **Corfu**). There is horseback riding (at Athens, Salonica, and on Crete). Several of the major resort hotels offer waterskiing, and many public beaches now have paddleboats and surfsails for rent. And Greek youths can usually be found playing informal games of soccer (football) or basketball: if you ask, you could probably join in. See also Mountaineering, Swimming, Tennis, Underwater Sports, Yachting.

SWIMMING: Swimming- or at least sunbathing is perhaps the main attraction for many visitors to Greece, and there are almost limitless beaches. In fact, though, not all Greek beaches are as sandy as you might wish. Inquire if you have a strong preference and a choice as to where the sandy beach is located. Likewise, not all beaches are as clean as you might wish- although if you get away from a city or built-up area the water should be perfectly clean and clear. What you cannot always escape-anywhere in the Mediterranean - is the tar that washes ashore and gets into the sand: a beach may look perfectly clean. but as you walk along the sand your feet pick up the buried tar. (This is one reason many people have taken to bringing flexible mats to the beaches: to save their towels from getting fouled). The usual precautions about avoiding undertows and un- expected currents should be observed. Many cities operate public beach facilities-chang- ing rooms, showers, etc. Nu- dist beaches are officially forbidden and in some areas local individuals actively seek to enforce the ban; in some places, if it is done with discretion, it will be ignored. Lastly the Mediterranean is not the tropics, and most people find the swimming season lasts only from May through September.

TAXIS: Taxis remain relati- vely cheap in Greece. They can also be hard to hire during certain busy hours-and for that reason, Greeks often share taxis, each party paying the metered fare to their destination. There is a mini- mum fare, too-no matter how short the distance. There may also be some surcharges be- yond the metered fare: for night rides, for certain holi- days, for luggage, to airports, etc. (Drivers should be able to indicate any such surcharges.) If it is to be an especially long trip, negotiate the fee before leaving. If it is to a remote locale and you want the driver to wait, there are set fees for waiting time. With two or more individuals sharing the cost, a taxi offers a reasonable way to make best use of a limited time in Greece.

TELEPHONES AND TE- LEGRAMS: In a few large cities, it has been traditional to use the phones available at many kiosks (or **periperterons**); you dial first and after you have completed your call you pay the proprietor. Now a large red telephone is replacing this system-and you must insert the coin first (it has for some time been a two-Drach- ma coin). Increasingly, too, phone booths are appearing all over Greece, and for these you need a two - Drachma coin. In some special phone booths you can even dial long distance, but most foreigners (as do most Greeks) will prefer to go to the office of the national phone company (**OTE**) and use the attended services. If you know-or can learn-the code numbers for your desired call, you can dial direct to virtually any place in the world. (Be persistent, though: the Greek phone system is good, but you must often try dialing several times to, make your connection). When you are finished with your call, you step over to the attendant who will read the 129 meter and provide you with a "bill". Since many Greeks still do not have telephones, these offices can be quite crowded at certain times, so go well in advance if you must place a call within a set period. Telegrams are sent from these same offices. The forms are printed in English as well as Greek, and the attendants are usually adept at dealing with foreigners' queries. Large hotels might be able to help you, too, with any special problems.

TENNIS: There are a fair number of tennis courts around Greece and most are open to non-Greeks (and non-members of the sponsoring clubs). Naturally the courts tend to be concentrated in a few areas-Athens (and its nearby beach resorts), large cities such as **Salonika** and **Patras,** and in the more popular holiday centers such as Crete, Rhodes, and Corfu. Inquire at offices of the **National Tourist Organization** for details; if tennis is a vital part of your holiday in Greece, you should make certain of arrangements before going to a particular locale.

THEFT: This is virtually a non-existent problem in Greece. Luggage can be left unattanded almost anywhere, purses or cameras can be forgotten at a restaurant-you will always find them waiting for you. On the other hand, it would be silly to leave a lot of currency or small valuables (jewels, watches, etc.) lying around in your hotel room: there are simply too many people passing through.

TIME: Greece is two hours ahead of **Greenwich Mean** 130 **Time** (that is, **London's** time).

Greece now observes **Summer Time** (in which clocks are set one hour ahead) on the same schedule as its fellow **Common Market** members. As for time during the Greek day, Greeks do not concern themselves much with punctuality. Beyond that, when they say "tomorrow morning", they may mean at 12 noon; "this afternoon" may well mean 4 PM. Make a fixed appointment, by all means, but do not get excited if it isn't kept to the minute.

TIPPING: Greeks used to consider it as beneath their dignity to accept tips, but the influx of foreign tourists has changed all that. Even so, by including the service charges in restaurant bills and hotel bills, Greeks try to eliminate some of the awkwardness involved in tipping. It is customary to give the waiter at least some "rounded off" change (e.g. the 15 Drachmas over a 385 Drachma bill); coins left on the table will go to the waterboy if there has been one. If you have had some personal contact or asked special services of personnel in your hotel, it is certainly not out of line to present a tip. Barbers, hairdressers, shoeshiners, and ushers (in movies as well as theaters) traditionally get modest tips. Taxi drivers are not supposed to expect tips, but you can expect a less than gracious smile if you do not at least give a small sum over the fare.

TOILETS: Hotels that most foreigners now stay in have modern toilet facilities (although the plumbing may look a bit exotic). Many of the older restaurants and tavernas, however, have quite primitive toilets: if you are squeamish about this, use your hotel toilet before going out to eat. There are public toilets (the attendants expect a tip) in all medium sized to large Greek cities-but they are often fairly primitive, too. Most of the better hotels have separate toilet facilities for their patrons, and if you look as though you belong you can usually make use of them.

TRAVELERS CHECKS: All the better known travelers checks are honored in banks, hotels, restaurants that cater to foreigners, and tourist gift shops. Do not expect every little corner store or village taverna, however, to accept a travelers check: buy your Drachmas before setting off for the countryside. See also CREDIT CARDS and BANKS.

UNDERWATER SPORTS: SCUBA diving is generally forbidden in Greek waters-the exception being in certain areas and under some supervision. (This restriction is because the Greeks fear that too many divers could lead to losses of their antiquities still to be found around the coasts.) Inquire at the National Tourist Organization for specifics. However, snorkeling (that is, with just a breathing tube, mask, and flippers) is allowed (as is fishing with a speargun, so long as it is not close to swimmers: See FISHING).

VILLAS FOR RENT: It is relatively easy-if expensive!-to rent completely furnished villas in many of the more popular holiday locales a-round Greece. (Villas, by the way, are distinguished from "houses" in that the former usually are out of the main residential areas and usually have a bit of land). Many villas are now rented only through various travel agents or firms specializing in such rentals: inquire of the National Tourist Organization or of major travel agents. Villas can be very expensive during the main season, but if several people are sharing the cost and make a fair number of meals at home, a villa can end up being relatively cheap.

VISAS: See PASSPORTS AND VISAS

WATER: The water of Greece is safe to drink in virtually any place the average traveler will be. (If foreigners sometimes complain of minor stomach ailments when traveling in Greece, it probably is not the water; in any case, it may be little more than a shift from one water to another-the type of upset one could experience in moving from any city to another). The fresh cold water from a natural spring is one of the delights of Greece. If you are truly sensitive, of course, you can always drink bottled water. A more realistic problem might be to get hot water whenever you want it in your hotel: ask beforehand to find out if hot water is provided at only certain hours.

YACHTING: There are numerous firms that rent yachts-mostly with crews - and this has become a popular way to tour Greece. They are undoubtedly expensive at first hearing, but if the cost is divided among several people, and then ho- 131 tels, other transportation, and at least some meals are being eliminated, the end result is not that expensive. These yachts come in all sizes, with or without sail, and with greater or lesser degrees of luxury. Inquire of the National Tourist Organization or major travel agents for more details.

YOUTH HOSTELS: SEE HOSTELS

ZOOS: For those people who like to round out their view of a foreign land by visiting the local zoo, Greece offers nothing truly worthy of that name. Athens, however, does have a modest display of animals in the National Garden, and it offers the advantage of being central and a convenient retreat from the heat and bustle of the city. And many Greek cities maintain small collections of animals in their public parks-often including some of the less familiar species of Greece such as the famous wild goat of Crete. Inquire of the local **Tourist Police** if you enjoy such diversions.

7 A little Greek for travelers

A	α	(álfa)	As in far.
B	β	(víta)	Closer to a soft v than to b.
Γ	γ	(gámma)	Before a, o, u: **gh**. Before e, i: **y**.
Δ	δ	(dhélta)	Closer to **dh** than to hard **d**.
E	ε	(épsilon)	As in sell.
Z	ζ	(zíta)	As in zeal.
H	η	(íta)	As in machine.
Θ	θ	(thíta)	As in theater.
I	ι	(jóta)	As in machine.
K	κ	(káppa)	As in kit.
Λ	λ	(lámdha)	As in lamp.
M	μ	(mí)	As in mit.
N	ν	(ní)	As in not.
Ξ	ξ	(xí)	As **ks** sound (as in extra)
O	o	(ómikron)	As in oar.
Π	π	(pí)	As in pit.
P	ρ	(ró)	As in red.
Σ	σ	ς(sígma)	As in sit.
T	τ	(táf)	As in tap.
Y	υ	(ípsilon)	As in machine.
Φ	φ	(fí)	As in fish.
X	χ	(chí)	A **kh** sound (as in **Khan**).
Ψ	ψ	(psí)	A **ps** sound (as in apse).
Ω	ω	(oméga)	As in ode.

BASIC DAILY SITUATIONS

Yes	né
Yes indeed!	málista
No	óchi
Greetings!	chérete!
Good morning	kaliméra
Good evening	kalispéra
Good night	kaliníkta
Stay well!	sto kaló
Excuse me	me sinchoríte **or** signómi!
Please	parakaló
Thank you	efcharistó
Not at all	típota
How are you	Ti kánete? **or** pos páte?
Very well	polí kalá
Do you speak English?	Miláte angliká?
I don't understand	Dhen katalavéno
What is that called?	Pos to léne aftó?
How do you say that	Pos to léne aftó
in Greek?	sta ellhniká?
What is your name?	Pos sas léne?
My name is-	Me léne-
Mister	kírios
Mrs.	kiría
Child	pedhí
Much	polí
Little	lígho
Over	epáno
Under	káto
There	ekí
Here	edó
Big	megálos
Little	mikrós

NUMBERS

1	éna	18	dhekaoktó
2	dhío	19	dhekaenéa
3	tría	20	íkossi
4	téssara	21	ikosiéna
5	pénte	30	triánda
6	éxi	40	saránda
7	eftá	50	penínda
8	októ	60	exínda
9	enéa	70	evdomínta
10	dhéka	80	ogdhónda
11	éndheka	90	eneninda
12	dódheka	100	ekató
13	dhekatría	200	diakóssia

133

14 dhekatéssera	300 triakóssia
15 dhekapénde	1000 khília
16 dhekaéxi	2000 dhío khiliádes
17 dhekaeftá	

TIME

Morning	to proí
Midday	to messiméri
Afternoon	to apóyevma
Evening	to vrádhi
Night	i níkhta
Yesterday	chtés
Today	símera
Tomorrow	ávrio
Early	enorís
Late	argá
When?	Póte?
Four o'clock (AM)	Stis tésseres to proí
At 5:30 PM	Stis pendémisi to apóyevma
Sunday	Kiriakí
Monday	Dheftéra
Tuesday	Tríti
Wednesday	Tetárti
Thursday	Pémpti
Friday	Paraskeví
Saturday	Sávato
Hour	óra
Day	iméra
Week	evdhomádha
Month	mínas
Year	chrónos

HOTEL

Hotel	xenodhokhío
Room	dhomátio
Bathroom	bánio
Bed	kreváti
Cover	kouvérta
Pillow	maxilári
Lamp	lámba
Cold water	krío neró
Hot water	zestó neró
Key	klidhí
Guest	xénos
Do you have a room with 2 beds?	Échete éna dhíklino dhomátio?
I am staying only one night	Tha míno mía níkhta

Can I pay with a credit card?	Boró na pliróso me aftí ti pistotikí kárta?
Do you accept travelers' checks?	Pérnete travellers checks?

RESTAURANTS

Restaurant	estiatório
Food	fayitó
Table	trapézi
Chair	karékla
Napkin	petséta
Plate	piáto
Cup	flitzáni
Glass	potíri
Fork	piroúni
Spoon	koutáli
Knife	machéri
Waiter	garsóni
Waterboy	mikrós
Check	loghariasmós
Tip	pourboire
Menu	katáloghos
Hors d'oeuvres	orektiká
Bread	psomí
Water	neró
Wine	krassí
Beer	bíra
Milk	ghála
Meat	kréas
Fish	psária
Chicken	kotópoulo
Hot	zestós
Cold	kríos

AROUND TOWN

Street	othós
Square	platía
Boulevard	leofóros
Attention!	Prossochí!
Forbidden	Apaghorévete
Open	aniktós
Shut	klistós
Entrance	íssodhos
Exit	éxodhos
Toilet	toualéta
Women	ghynekón
Men	andhrón
Store	maghazí
Kiosk	períptero

135

Post office	takhidhromío
Letter	ghrámma
Stamp	grammatósimo
Airmail	aeroporikós
Telephone	tiléfono
Telegram	tilegráfima
How much does it cost?	Póso káni aftó?
Bank	trápeza
Money	khrímata
Drachmas	drachmés
I would like to exchange a check	Thélo na aláxo éna tsek.
Laundry	plidirio
Dry-cleaning	katharistírio
I need it tommorow	Prépi na íne étimo ávrio to proí

ON THE ROAD

Automobile	aftokínito
Bus	leoforío
Taxi	taxi
Motorcycle	motosikléta
Bicycle	podhílato
Ship	plío **or** karávi
Airplane	aeropláno
Railroad station	stathmós trénou
Stop(bus)	stássi
Map	khártis
Ticket	issitírio
Gas station	pratírion venzínis
Gas	venzíni
Oil	ládhi
Kilometer	khiliómetro
Straight ahead	kat efthían
Right	dhexiá
Left	aristerá
Opposite	apénandi
One way	apló
Roundtrip (return)	me epistrofí
Quickly	grígora
Slowly	sighá
Where is-?	Pou íne?-
How many hours?	Pósses óres?
When does the bus leave?	Ti óra févyi to leoforío?

INDEX

A little Greek for travelers 132
Accommodations on Rhodes 57
Achaia 104
Activities and diversions 59
Aegean 9
Aesclepius 12
Afandou 90
Agama stellio 17, 46
Ahmed Hafouz Library 75
Air travel 112
Alimnia 106
Alphabet 112
Amboise Gate 74
American coffee 119
Americans 118
An Introduction 9
Animal life 17
Antiquities 112
Aphrodite of Rhodes 70
Aphrodite Thalassia 70
Apolakia 107
Aragon 70
Aretsínoto 120
Arkhangelos 92
Armaldo Gate 82
Around town 135
Arsenal square 65
Artillery Gate 74
Asklipion 107
Athens 112
Athens area 118
Automobile club 112
Average monthly temperatures in
  centigrade 15
Avis 114
Ayios Nikolaos 27

Babysitters 113
Banks 113
Barbers 113
Basic daily situations 133

Bathing 113
BBC 127
Bicycles for rent 113
Boating 34
Bus travel 113

California 118
Camping 114
Car rental 114
Casino 61
Castille 70
Castle of Monolithos 107
Cathedral 63
Chalki 9
Charter Cruises 114
Church of St. John 102
Churches 115
Cigarettes and cigars 115
Clean Monday 118
Clock Tower 74
Clothing 115
Collachium 65
Common Market 130
Complaints 115
Constantinople 114
Consulates and Embassies 116
Copenhai 44
Corfu 128
Council of the order 70
Crafts and shopping 40
Credit Cards 116
Crete 27
Crowds 21
Crusader 12
Customs Control 116
Cycladic islands 115

Del Carretto's 86
Dentists 116
Dimoglou Nelly 38
Dionysos 39

Directorate of Antiquities 127
Doctors 117
Dodeca 9
Dodecannese 9
Driving in Greece 117
Drugs 118
Drycleaning 118

Earthquakes 118
East Air Terminal 112
Easter 118
Easter Sunday 118
Eating and drinking 42
Electricity 118
Ellenikós kafés 119
ELPA 112
Embassies 118
England 70
Ephesus 114
Epta Pighes 92
European 118

Faliraki 58, 90
Ferula Chiliantha 18
Festivals 36
Fishing 33, 119
Fishing and Hunting 35, 60
Folegandros 27
Food and Drink 119
Formation of the Dodecannese
 islands 13
France 70
French coffee 119

Gate of Liberty 65
General Delivery 126
General Practical Information
 from A to Z 112
Gennadi 60, 107
Germany 70
Getting around Rhodes 57
Glykó 120
Golf and Tennis 59
Good Friday 118
Government House of the
 Knights 102

Grand Master 70
Greek Easter 118
Greek Embassies 123
Greek islands 114
Greek language 120
Greek Mountainclimbing Club
 125
Greek Youth Hostels Assoccia-
 tion 122
Greenwich Mean Time 130
Guides and Interpreters 121

Hairdressers 121
Halikarnassos 49
Halki 27
Haraki 92
Helios 62
Hertz 114
Hippocrates 12
Hippocrates square 81
Hippocratic Oath 12
Hitchhiking 121
Holidays 121
Hospice of St. Catherine 82
Hospital of the Knights 69
Hospitality 122
Hospitals 122
Hostels 122
Hotels 57, 132, 123, 134
Hours 123
House of Papas Konstandinos 99
Hunting 33, 123
Hyoscyamus aureus 18

Ialysos 46, 103, 104
Information 123
International Driver's License
 114
Ionian islands 115
Ios 27
Italian Tower 86
Italian Tower belonged 85
Italy 70, 118

Jewish Passover 118

138

Kalamaria 42
Kalathos 92
Kallithea 60, 110
Kalolimni 36
Kameiros 46, 103, 104
Karpathos 9, 27
Kassos 27
Kastellorizo 110
Kastellos 106
Katavia 107
Khurmale Medresses 75
Knidos 49
Kolymvia 92
Koskinou 85, 90
Kremasti 104
Kretinae 106
Kritinia 106
Ksifies 42

Ladhi 119
Laundry 124
Lent 118
Leros 9, 30
Lindos 46, 90
Lipsoi 9
Lithospermum fruticosum 18
Lithrini 42
Lost Atlantis 118
Luggage 124

Malona 92
Mandraki 62
Marine Gate 82
Marithes 42
Martyrs' Square 82
Me olighi 120
Medicines 124
Megisti 9
Meltemi 16, 21
Menu 124
Métrios 120
Mezedháki 119
Mezés 119
Milos 27
Money 124
Monolithos 107

Mosque of Aga 81
Motorbikes for rent 124
Mountaineering and Walking 35
Mountaineering 60, 125
Moussaká 120
Movies 125
Mt. Acramitis 45
Mt. Atavyros 36
Mt. Lastos 36
Mt. Profitis Elias 36
Municipal Theater 63
Music and Dance 60

National Tourist Organization 34
National Archaeological Service
   112
Naxos 27
New Market 63
New Town 62
Newspapers and magazines 125
Nisyros 9, 14, 30
Numbers 133

Octopothi keftethes 42
Old Town 62
Olympic Airways 112
On the road 136
Orektika 119
OTE 129
Other sites on Rhodes 103
Othos Apollonion 75
Our Lady of victory 82
Oúzo 120

Paeonia Rhodia 18
Pagotá 119
Palace of the Castellan 81, 82
Palace of the Grand Masters 74, 85
Panayia 99
Panayia Katholiki 92
Pangaea 13
Parking 125
Paros 27
Passports and Visas 126
Patani 38
Patmos 9, 30

Patras 116, 130
Pensions 126
Peripterons 129
Petaloudhes (Valley of the Butter-
flies) 103
Pharmacies 126
Photography 126
Pindar Street 82
Piraeus 116
Plaki 42
Plant Life 17
Police 126
Post Office 126
Poste Restante 126
Preface 9
Prices 126
Professional entertainment 40
Profitis Elias 108
Protestants Churches 115
Protestants in Greece 115
Provence Auvergne 70

Radio 127
Reduction 127
Religion 127
Restaurants 58, 127, 135
Revelation 12
Rhodes 9, 45, 112
Rhodes: old town 65
Rhodes in myth and history 46
Rhodini 90
Rhodon 45
Roman Catholics in Greece 115
Rooms to rent 128

Samos 57
Sanctuary of Athena Lindia 102
Santorini 14, 27
School of Rhetoric of Aeschines
90
Ships and airplanes to Rhodes 56
Shopping and souvenirs 122
Sailing 128
Sitia 27
Skala 116
Skala Kameiros 106

Skétos 120
Sound and light 60
Southern Sporades 9
Spain 70
Spanish tower 85
Sporades 9
Sports 33, 128
St. Catherine's gate 86
St. George's Tower 85
St. John's 85
St. John's church 72
St. Mary's tower 85
St. Nicholas 63
Suleiman square 74, 79
Suleiman's mosque 74
Summer time 130
Swimming 33, 129
Swimming and sunbathing 33
Swimming and watersports 59
Syme 9

Taxis 129
Telephones and telegrams 129
Telos 9
Temple of Pythian Apollo 65
Temple to Athena 103
Tennis 33, 130
Tennis and golf 34
The Athenian 125
The Athens News 125
The city of Rhodes 62
The climate of the Dodecannese
15
The drive to Lindos 90
The Medieval walls of Rhodes 84
The Physical environment 13
The Physical presence 45
The Spoken language 120
The twelve 9
The Written language 120
Theft 130
Thessaloniki 115
Tethys Sea 13
Time 134
Time for the Dodecannese 23
Tinos 30

140

Tipping 130
Toilets 130
Tongue of Auvergne 68
Tourist Police 113, 118
Tower of Naillac 82, 85, 86
Tower of St. Mary 85
Traditional popular culture 38
Travelers cheques 130
Traveling around the Dodecanne-
  se 26
Traveling to and on Rhodes 56
Travelling on the Dodecannese 31
Trianda 103
Tsambouna 38
Turkey 114

Underwater Sports 33, 131
Underwater Swimming 34
UNESCO 127

Valley of the butterflies 104

Villas for rent 131
Visas 131
Visiting Dodecannese 20
Voice of America 127

Water 131
Watersports 34
Weather 20
West Air Terminal of Athens'
  Hellinikon Airport 112
Western Christian Easter 118
Western Christian churches 118
Wine Festival 61
Wrapping up your visit to the city
  of Rhodes 86

Yachting 33, 131
Youth Hostels 132

Zoos 132